IF you're going to San Francisco, be sure to wear a flower in your hair.

R Lowe,
Norwich

SMOKERS. If using chewing gum as part of your effort to kick the habit, check that the packet does not say 'Contains a source of phenyalanine. Excessive consumption may produce laxative effects' before chewing your way through three packets in one day.

Mr Shittypants,
Edinburgh

GIVE up smoking by sticking one cigarette from each new pack up a fat friend's arse, filter first, then replacing it in the box. The possibility of putting that one in your mouth will put you off smoking any of them.

Harold Fletcher,
Maiden Castle

PUT on a pair of swimming trunks and ask your wife to hit you over the head with a chair and push you through a pasting table. Get your kids to boo and chant obscenities and hey presto! You're the star of your own WWF wrestling show.

Bob Harris,
Cardiff

OFFICE managers. When leaving your office desk for any length of time, make sure you leave your mobile phone on and unattended. Set it to play The Yellow Rose of Texas at high volume, instead of just ringing, then complain loudly when you return and find it in pieces in the bin.

Damian O'Neil,
Heaton

READ Exchange and Mart from cover to cover whilst sitting on the toilet. When you eventually get up and try to walk on your numbed legs you will find your legs swaying and gyrating, just like Elvis.

F. Starr,
A pub somewhere

THROW large, peeled carrots into your garden pond. They are indistinguishable from expensive Koi carp.

F.W. Adey,
Wolverhampton

STOP birds nesting in your garden by collecting all the twigs and moss in your neighbourhood and hiding it in your garden shed.

P. Reaney,
Rothwell

TORIES. Avoid wear and tear on your vocal chords when asked about poverty by simply shrugging your shoulders.

Hans Clap,
e-mail

FROZEN sprouts are a tasty alternative to boiled sweets. And they don't rot kids' teeth.

Mrs F. Penn,
Burnley

Compiled and edited by
Graham Dury, Davey Jones and Simon Thorp

Designed by
Alex Morris

Viz would like to thank all the readers over the years who have sent in their Top Tips. Ta.

Top Tips appear every 5 weeks in Viz Comic, available in newsagents, supermarkets, petrol stations and a big skip out the back of the printers. To subscribe in the UK, phone 0844 844 0380. For overseas subscriptions (excluding USA & Canada), phone +44 (0)1795 592 924 or fax: +44 (0)1795 414 555. For USA & Canada subscriptions: 1-888-428-6676 or fax 1-757-428-6253, or visit www.viz.co.uk. Digital subscriptions (on PC, Mac, Android, iPad, iPhone and Major Morgan) are available at zinio.com and Apple Newsstand. You can submit a Top Tip by post to **Viz Comic, PO Box 841, Whitley Bay, NE26 9EQ**; by email to **toptips@viz.co.uk**; by twitter to **twitter.com/vizcomic**, or via **www.viz.co.uk**.

First published 2012 by Dennis Publishing Ltd., 30 Cleveland Street, London W1T 4JD. Distributed by Pan Macmillan Ltd.

ISBN 978-1781060919

A CIP catalogue record for this book is available from the British Library, but you'll have to be very quiet when you ask for it because there's people trying to read.

Printed in the United Kingdom.

WHEN carrying a cup of tea from one room to another always add a spoonful of cornflower. This will thicken it up and prevent it from spilling over the rim and onto the carpet.

**Mrs E. Davis,
Blackpool**

FUMES from burning settees can be lethal so before sitting down always look around and plan your escape route in the event of a fire.

**D. Pumell,
Bristol**

CREATE a perfect pond for small gardens by burying an old saucepan and filling it with water. Add an upturned soda syphon and hey presto! An ornamental fountain.

**G. Wilmot,
Edmundbyers**

I'D imagine that shorter, thinner lengths of wire connecting appliances to the mains will probably reduce the amount of electricity they use.

**Peter Redman,
Devizes**

WHY waste money on first class stamps? Simply write your letters a few days earlier, and send them second class.

**P. Honk,
Leamington Spa**

DIY enthusiasts. Make your approach more professional by starting 3 days late, wearing ill-fitting trousers and shaking your head at regular intervals

**J. O'Reilly,
Stockport**

NORTHERNERS. Don't waste money on a day trip to London. Simply stay in your living room with the doors and windows closed and the heating on full until you can hardly breathe. Then get your neighbours to crack your shins with a brief case and stand on your toes at regular intervals.

**Pedro Morley,
e-mail**

I WEAR my husband's safety boots with steel toe caps when removing tea bags from a cup, as they invariably drip hot water.

**N. Coquet (Mrs),
Surrey**

DON'T throw away old socks with holes in the toe. Simply cut off the whole toe, turn the sock around and sew up the other end. Hey presto! A new sock.

**A. White,
Kettering**

WHEN reaching down to pick up dropped cutlery beneath the kitchen table I always wear my husband's motorcycle crash helmet as I invariably bump my head on the table whilst getting up again.

**N. Coquet (Mrs),
Surrey**

WHEN cooking bacon I wear my husband's welding mask and leather apron to protect myself from the spitting fat.

**N. Coquet (Mrs),
Surrey**

Mr Fred Astaire's
TAP TIPS

SPECTACLE wearers. Rid yourself of cumbersome spectacles by getting a pair of contact lenses. To stop them falling out from time to time, take a length of brass wire, create a figure-8 shape and loop it around the outer rim of each contact lens. For added security, leave an extra length of wire protruding each side that can be used to hold the frame in place by hooking it round your ears.

**Stewart,
Cowley**

WHEN asked if you have any questions at a job interview, increase your chances of getting the job by asking the interviewer, or the whole panel in turn where they get their hair cut.

**James James
e-mail**

DAILY MAIL reporters. Run a story on your website about how appalling it is that a pervy landlord installed hidden cameras to spy on unsuspecting teenage students. Then follow it with a 'showbiz' story about Miley Cyrus wearing a bikini, illustrated with lots of photos of her in the bikini, taken from a long way away without her knowledge.

**Nicko,
Australia**

DENTAL floss makes an ideal noose for depressed ants wishing to hang themselves from the branches of a bonsai tree.

**Hasto,
e-mail**

PREGNANT weatherwomen. When presenting the report, stand front on to the camera so as anybody living west of Stoke on Trent can see what the weather will be like in their area.

**Heppy,
West Yorks**

STRESSED-OUT office bosses. Cover your knackers with tin foil and hit the side of one of them with a hammer. Hey presto! A cheap yet effective 'Newton's Cradle'-type executive toy.

**A. Beech,
Newcastle**

PREVENT getting lost on forest walks by scattering a trail of breadcrumbs behind you. When you decide to go home, simply follow the trail all the way back.

H & G,
Bavaria

ACTORS. Improve your chances of landing a role in a Tim Burton film by being Helena Bonham-Carter.

Ted Bartlett,
e-mail

IF a dog is about to attack you in the street, stand your ground. Do not show any sign of fear, as this would encourage the animal to attack.

Mrs B. Sellers,
Cricklewood

AVOID being murdered, raped, held hostage in a siege, poisoned, stabbed to death and buried under a patio, blown up by religious extremists, falling victim to a fatal mystery virus, embroiled in a drug war, burgled, falsely imprisoned, blackmailed and probably murdered again by simply not moving to one of the seven houses in Brookside Close.

P. Redmond,
Liverpool

DON'T panic when being chased overland by a crocodile. Simply run in a zig-zag fashion. These large reptiles are only able to run in straight lines and will be confused by your constant changes in direction. Soon he will give up the chase.

Mrs B. Sellers,
Cricklewood

FOIL fiddling taxi drivers by taking polaroid photographs of street signs as you pass them. At the end of the journey you can confront him with photographic evidence if he has taken an unnecessarily long route.

R. Holmes,
Putney

HALF a horse chestnut conker shell would make a frightening hat for a tortoise.

P. Beetroot,
Cubbard

SECOND rate Scottish female celebrities. When flying from London to Glasgow on a Friday night, always board last and make an awful fuss about the lockers being full, thus ensuring everyone seated will know who you are. Better still, stop fucking around with pots of paint in other people's houses and get a proper job.

Barry Turnbull,
e-mail

BUS DRIVERS. If you see an attractive woman with a low cut top at the bus stop, accelerate and come to a halt fifty feet past the stop. You will then have a great view in your nearside mirror as she runs towards you. Finally, accidentally drop her change for a second look.

A. Driver,
Bolton

CREATE your own cash dispenser by lying your toaster on its side. Put £50 in ironed banknotes in one slot, then enter your bank card in the other. Then set the toaster. After a short while 'pop!' Out comes your cash, together with your returned card. (Always use a low setting to prevent your money from catching fire or your card from melting.)

K. Carr,
London SW 1

PUT paid to the expression 'the grass is always greener on the other side of the fence' by having your lawn concreted over.

B. Bounty,
Rochester

KEEP monkeys out of your kitchen by hiding bananas on top of a wardrobe in your bedroom.

Mrs D. Includes-Underlay,
Andfitting

Top Tips

SSERS.
bid cunt
fucki
ankin
for
nd
vo
n

CYCLISTS. Tie a paint brush loaded with yellow paint to the end of your right hand handlebar. This will mark any car that passes too close and allow the police to easily identify the offenders.
Frank Bugle, e-mail

WOMEN. When arguing with your boyfriend that you are the more logical of the species, do not then go and buy clothes that do up round the back.
Phillip Smith, e-mail

RIOTERS. Wear at top hat and shout 'Buller! Buller! Buller!' whilst causing criminal damage to prevent the Prime Minister, the Lord Mayor of London and the Chancellor of the Exchequer from criticising your actions.
T Thorn, Hexham

SLIGHTLY overweight women. Look and feel like you are Kate Moss by moving to Worksop.
Simon Burdett, e-mail

PEOPLE on the right. If you would prefer to wap bam boogie, please ensure you move to the left, otherwise you may have to boogaloo instead.
Simon Conroy, e-mail

PETER Andre. Save money when ordering tailored shirts by not ordering the first 5 buttons, (or first 4 buttons for winter shirts).
Dan Waite, e-mail

COACH passengers. When travelling abroad, always pack your passport near the top of your suitcase, and ask the driver to leave it handy near the front of the boot. This greatly reduces the time spent rummaging around for it at border crossings etc.

K. Dee,
Monaco

WHEN using cash dispensing machines it is possible to prevent the person behind you from knowing your number by deliberately keying in the wrong one. Then pretend to collect your money, and walk away smiling innocently.

A. Walker,
Nottingham

BBC 6Music breakfast presenter Shaun Keaveny. Go to bed a little earlier. Then you won't have to spend half of your show grumpily moaning on about how tired you are. By definition, your listeners are up and about, and unlike you they don't get to knock off work at 10 in the morning.

T. S. Ball,
Leeds

PROLONG the life of your carpets by rolling them up each night before bed and storing them in the shed.

R Babbington,
e-mail

MAKE 'thick' stamps costing only two pence by filing a 2p piece into a rectangular shape and painting it red.

R. Yarwood,
Runcorn

SAINSBURYS directors. Attract more people into your stores by not getting Jamie Oliver to do your adverts, and using the money to make your beans and stuff a bit cheaper.

J. Geils,
Wrexham

LADIES. Cycling helmet too big? Place a panty-liner inside the rim for a snug fit. (But don't use the ones with wings or you'll look like Deputy Dawg).

Janet Forrest,
Kendal

CREATE your own 'boil-in-the-bag' cod in parsley sauce by scraping the breadcrumbs off a fish finger and placing it inside a used condom.

E. Evans,
Evesham

GARDENERS. Take a tip from fashion designers. Paint long, thin parallel lines on your garden hose to give the impression that it is longer than it actually is. Or paint thicker hoops along its length to create a new, shorter look.

Percy Bike,
Huddersfield

DEFY the government at the start of British Summer Time by refusing to put your clocks forward at 2.00 in the morning. 'Save' the hour for later in the day. You still get your lie-in and you can fast forward your day when it suits you, like when there is nothing on telly.

Terry Davenport,
e-mail

10

WHITE wine splashed onto a red wine stain will clean it up quickly. Similarly, fat splashes on clothes can be easily removed by rubbing salad onto the affected area.

Rick Stein, Padstow

WHEN it stops raining, run to the nearest car park. By counting the number of dry patches you can work out how many cars have left the car park since the rain stopped.

H. Dingle, London

SIMILARLY, by looking underneath all the cars and counting the number of vehicles with wet tarmac below them, you can work out how many cars have arrived since the rain stopped.

H. Dingle, London

THE TOTAL of the two figures represents the net traffic flow through the car park's entrance/exit in the moments since precipitation ceased.

H. Dingle, London

UNFORTUNATELY any car which arrived after the rain stopped, and parked on a recently vacated dry space, would not be accountable by this method.

H. Dingle, London

WHEN travelling by train jot down a note of any refreshments you require and pin it to your lapel. This will save you having to talk to the miserable bastard who is invariably serving in the buffet car.

P. Donnelly, Portsmouth

PREVENT cats from eating the contents of your fridge while they are standing on your doorstep by surrounding them with chicken wire.

L. Lipton, Lanarkshire

MURDERERS. Avoid 'capital' punishment by committing your crimes in provincial cities such as Manchester.

F. Grunblatt, Sunderland

FARTING in bed a problem? Before you hit the sack, try popping a Mint Imperial up your Marmite motorway. That way your guffs will smell good enought to eat.

Sue Denim, London

GENTS. After visiting the barber, remove hairs from the back of your neck by inflating a balloon, rubbing it on your jumper in order to charge it with static electricity, and then gently brushing it along the collar line and around your ears.

B. Derby-Hatt, Luton

A STRING of sausages draped across the room makes an ideal edible Christmas decoration. But be sure to cook them before giving them to the kids.

**Mrs I. Jones,
Hebden Bridge**

CONVINCE neighbours that you have an expensive alarm by locking your car and then making loud, high pitched 'whooping' noises as you walk away.

**S. Black,
Burnley**

SHOPPERS. Take the legwork out of shopping by simply standing at the supermarket check-out and removing any items you require from other people's trolleys as they approach.

**S. O'Keefe,
Waterford**

GIRLS. Get those old 70's bell-bottoms from the wardrobe, cut the legs off and sew them back on upside down. They will then fit you once more.

**Andy Balkham,
Wandsworth**

GIRLS. Practise being an air hostess by standing up at the end of the aisle and demonstrating emergency landing procedures every time you get on a bus.

**Mrs Joyce Clooney,
Littlehampton**

KIDS. Hide single-serving tomato sauce sachets under your Action Man's clothing to add extra realism when he is bayonetted or stabbed during play battles.

**Y. Gray,
Evesham**

CONVERT black labrador dogs into seals by feeding them pastries, sweets and cakes, starving them of exercise, slipping a pair of black socks onto their front paws and smearing their coats in vaseline. Then encourage them to balance a beach ball on their nose in return for fish-shaped dog biscuits.

**R. Crosbie,
Cheltenham**

FAIRY Liquid bosses. Dilute your washing up liquid with water. Then you won't need to spend so much money on TV adverts telling people how strong it is.

**Y. Bell,
Norfolk**

WHENEVER you're shot in the chest, lie on the side you were hit. That way only one lung will fill with blood.

**Major G. Symonds,
Codsall**

POWER station managers. Paint your chimneys white with orange and yellow bases to make it look like the ground is enjoying a cigarette. When the chimney is eventually demolished, ask the demolition men to paint it grey, beginning at the top and progressing downwards, occasionally 'flicking' off the tip using a demolition ball and chain, into a giant ashtray.

**John Gray,
Keighley**

MUMS. Add sparkling mineral water to a tin of condensed soup, then heat. Hey presto! Fizzy soup that your kids will adore.

**Rowland Lee,
Nottingham**

GARDENERS. Impatient waiting for your new trees to grow? Why not simply buy small trees in a pot, and place them on top of telegraph poles?

**M. Kinghorn,
Sudbury**

WHEN being photographed for a bus pass or railcard, wear a large hat, sun glasses and a big false moustache. The card can then be lent for use by any of your friends, along with the hat, sunglasses and false moustache.

**John Harkness,
Kesslemere**

TOFF TIPS

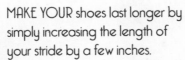

MAKE YOUR shoes last longer by simply increasing the length of your stride by a few inches.
Miss L. Parish.
Armley

DENTICAL twins. Use Morse code to cheat in exams by stabbing yourself in the arm with a sharp compass. The other twin, at home with a text book, can 'feel' the question and stab you back the answers.
W. Walker.
Norwich

MUMS. Out of Christmas wrapping paper? Simply convert birthday wrapping paper by adding "Jesus" after "Happy Birthday."
Roll Fizzlebeef.
e-mail

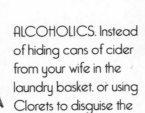

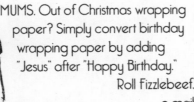

ALCOHOLICS. Instead of hiding cans of cider from your wife in the laundry basket, or using Clorets to disguise the smell of vomit from your boss, use your deviousness and intellect for greater financial reward by becoming a criminal mastermind like Lex Luther or Ernst Blofeld.
Dave Storey.
e-mail

HAVE fun in the supermarket next time you go alcohol shopping. Fill your trolley to bursting point with booze, then add one packet of nappies. When paying, pretend that you don't have enough money and put the nappies back. Watch the faces of the checkout personnel. Priceless.
Wax.
Addlestone

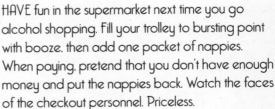

FOOL women into thinking their opinions are valued by nodding occasionally and saying "mmm".
Stu Holt.
South Shields

AMERICANS. Wipe out the Iraqi insurgency by simply joining their side. With your 'friendly fire' tactics, the war should be over in days.
Gaz.
e-mail

GUYS. If your lady's reluctant to swallow, make her eat haloumi cheese to get her used to the taste.

E.C. McG,
Canterbury

SUPERMARKETS. Sell your undersized vegetables for twice the price by not cleaning the shit off them and calling them 'organic'.

B. Cormack
Castle Douglas

FATHERS. If you have a new-born baby, never made a derogatory comment on your wife's skills as a mother.

Marc Johnson,
Palace Hotel,
Southend-on-Sea

BARMAIDS. Pour all my mates' lagers first, and THEN my Guinness, to ensure half my night is spent at the fucking bar.

Stu Holt,
South Shields

OLD LINGERIE from the Ann Summers shop can be re-used around the house as sexually-arousing dusters.

Lambert O'Butler,
Devizes

FATTIES. Take a tip from smokers and stop your cravings for chips by taping a crisp to the top of your arm each morning.

L. Zebra,
Chessington

TRAINLINE telephone employees. Retain an air of mystery by never giving accurate information.

Kelly Durkin,
e-mail

BLUE Peter presenters. Bring the old home-made toy telephone up to date by not using anything to join two paper cups together.

Twitchy John,
e-mail

MIDDLE-EASTERN dictators. Avoid having to destroy missiles capable of traveling 7 miles further than the 93-mile limit set by international law by simply agreeing to only ever launch them from 7 miles further back.

Jim Bailey,
Leeds

OLDER WOMEN. Don't spend a fortune on anti-ageing cosmetics as they will jeopardise your chances of being offered a seat on a bus.

Lord Wilberforce,
e-mail

NUNS at St Cuthbert's School in the early 1970s. Demonstrate a keen sense of irony by calling yourselves the 'Sisters of Mercy' whilst beating the shit out of us kids on a daily basis with bamboo canes.

Paul Bradshaw,
e-mail

HOUSEWIVES. Look in the dictionary to find the difference between the words 'need' and 'want', then carefully choose the right one to use when talking about buying new dresses.

Eggman,
e-mail

NICK Griffin. After stating that you find the sight of two men kissing in public creepy, add that you find the sight of two women kissing highly erotic. That way you cannot be accused of homophobia.

Alasdair Henry,
Newcastle

MAKE sure you get good service at the McDonald's Drive-thru by pasting a big yellow 'M' to your windscreen and ticking a clipboard as you place your order.

Rosslynman,
e-mail

WHEN NAILING your scrotum to a kitchen table for the purposes of sexual gratification, always ensure that you leave the pliers within arms' reach, not in your toolbox in the shed.

J Paxman,
London

LATE for work? Simply sneak in the side door and hide your coat in a drawer, then grab some paper from the photocopy room and casually walk to your desk pretending to read the blank sheets of paper.

Simon,
e-mail

WAIT till your neighbours get into their car, then fool them into thinking the handbrake doesn't work by pulling their house backwards.

Jimmy Docherty,
e-mail

THINKING of waterfalls and fountains is well known to help one urinate. Similarly, thinking of landslides and lorries unloading soil can help even the most constipated person clear their bowels.

Roger Green,
e-mail

CHINESE citizens. Improve chopstick performance by simply carving one into three points and fashioning a serrated edge on the other. Hey presto! No more chopstick based faux pas!

POB,
e-mail

MEN. Make sure that your lady always gets to sleep in the wet patch by ejaculating into her side of the bed before she gets into it.

Manytrix,
e-mail

REDUCE your tax bill by submitting your returns with the important parts blacked out, a la politicians' expense forms. Then just write £1.50 in the 'Tax Due' section at the bottom.

Lex Muir,
e-mail

SMOKERS. A sliver of chicken in the end of your cigarette turns an anti-social smell into an irresistible barbecue aroma, ensuring your popularity in public places.

Trevor Topsoil
e-mail

FOOL your neighbours into believing you somehow run a private harbour or port by blowing a low A on a baritone saxophone every 15 minutes and emitting high-pitched squeals to emulate seagulls.

Gregory Reuland,
e-mail

INHABITANTS of Putney. Instantly reduce the cost of your coffee at Cafe Nero near the tube station by 15%. Simply purchase a cappuccino "to go", then body swerve just before you reach the door and sit in that booth round the corner of the counter where the feckless staff never go.

S Cowley,
Putney

BMW drivers. When approaching a traffic jam on a motorway, feel free to do a last minute swerve into the lane I'm in, halving the braking distance I was allowing myself and putting the horses I was transporting on their fucking knees.

Nick,
Dorset

BEAT the credit crunch. When you hear your neighbour running a bath, get a friend to go round and distract them until the water comes over their overflow pipe. Then stand under it for a free hot shower.

Anton Seventies,
e-mail

VAT Inspectors. When carrying out spot checks on small businesses, refuse all offers of tea or coffee. It is not impossible that the proprietor may have wiped his cheesy knob all around the rim of the mug. I know I always do.

P. Roberts,
Holyhead

SKATEBOARDERS. Next time you come to a set of steps with a handrail in the middle, pick up your skateboard in one hand, grasp the handrail with the other and carefully walk down the steps. This way it won't be quite as painful on your bollocks.

Steve,
e-mail

SAVE money on batteries by only putting them into your clock when you wish to know the time.

Matthew Wilson,
e-mail

MOTHERS. Don't use poisonous shampoos on your children's hair to get rid of headlice. Scare them away using a dinner plate and an anglepoise lamp to cast a terrifying Independence Day-style shadow over your child's head.

A. Feather,
Caterham

ROMAN Polanski. Prevent your extradition from Switzerland by telling the Swiss authorities that you are made of solid gold.

Bill Decker,
e-mail

COMMUTERS. Give away the sad fact that your life consists of nothing but grinding routine by standing in the exact spot on the platform where the train doors will be when the service arrives.

Christina Martin,
e-mail

FOOL everyone into thinking you have just eaten an apple by rubbing your tummy and saying loudly "Mmm! That was a lovely apple."

Brian Clark,
e-mail

TOP CHIPS

MAKE your steam iron glide effortlessly over your clothes by filling it with vegetable oil instead of water.

Peter Sandlee, London

FATTIES. Avoid your torso being surreptitiously filmed and used in a BBC news report about Britain's obesity problem by always wearing a T-shirt with 'All Newsreaders are Cunts' written on it.

J Thorn, Hexham

MEN. Trick people into thinking you have washed your hands after going to the toilet by rubbing them under hot water with soap, then shaking them dry as you leave.

Simon Diamond, e-mail

MEN. Trick people into thinking you have washed your hands after going to the toilet by rubbing them under hot water with soap, then shaking them dry as you leave.

Simon Diamond, e-mail

SEAN Connery. Over-emphasise your Scottishness by rolling your Rs and occasionally wearing a kilt and nobody will remember that you haven't lived there for years.

GS Hickman, e-mail

YOUNG mothers. Calm hysterically crying children in the supermarket by firmly slapping their legs and then tugging them along by the wrist.

Jamie McKenzie, West Drayton

WALKERS. Use the phrase 'take on fluids' instead of 'drink water' to make it sound like you're conducting a fucking military expedition instead of going for a walk in some hills.

D Cooper, e-mail

TEENAGE boys. For accurate penis-length measurements, a button attached to a paper-clip makes an ideal miniature trundle wheel.

Tim Buck, Leamington Spa

« top tips »

FRUMPY middle-aged women. Save your energy by not lusting after Cliff Richard. I've worked back stage at his gigs and his cock is tiny.

N. Nurse, e-mail

WHEN very drunk and taking a shit, never under any circumstances stop to blow your nose when wiping your arse.

Marc Johnson, Leigh-on-Sea

CONVINCE neighbours that you own an old-fashioned typewriter by wearing metal thimbles and drumming your fingers on a plastic tray. Every ten seconds ting a wine glass with a pencil and run a butter knife along the teeth of a comb before continuing drumming your fingers.

E Tring, Luton

ZOOKEEPERS. Get round politically correct rules against holding chimps' tea parties by dressing bears up as chimps. This can be done using a grass skirt, a wig made of leaves and a couple of coconut shell quarters attached to their jaws. To make things go with a swing, put honey on the currant buns.

Johnny Pring, e-mail

TOURETTE'S sufferers with an interest in Victoriana. Simply replace shouting 'fuck', 'cunt' and 'wanker' with 'poppycock', 'fiddlesticks' and 'balderdash' to recreate an authentic Victorian experience.

S Nonsense, e-mail

A SIMPLE check that your wife has not accidentally left Flash toilet-wipes on top of the cistern instead of the usual Andrex moist bum-wipes will avoid cross words and marital discord.

Paul Berriman, e-mail

PUT a sawn-off piece of exhaust pipe in your mouth in an attempt to fool your Dad you've swallowed his car.

Ken Leopard, e-mail

SAVE time by only ever watching one Bruce Willis movie.

Zed, e-mail

FAT ladies. Eat cakes, pies, chocolates etc., using only the tips of your fingers so you look dainty.

Roy Aspinall, e-mail

CAR thieves. Don't be discouraged when nothing is on view. All the valuables may be hidden in the glove box or under a seat.

Tim, e-mail

MAKE people believe you are magic by vigorously shaking a bottle of talcum powder when you exit a room, thus giving the impression of you disappearing in a cloud of smoke.

Christopher Lou, Martinsville

JAMIE Oliver. When you bring out a new book, why not price it at £12 rather than £25? This would save the shops having to put 'Half Price' stickers on them before they go on the shelves.

Roland Butter, e-mail

STUDENTS. When asked to write a 3000-word essay, simply draw 3 pictures, as they are worth 1000 words each.

Peter E., e-mail

A FEW flat black and white pieces of Lego sandwiched together maker ideal liquorice allsorts for people who don't like eating them very much.

Claude Balls, e-mail

PARENTS. Each week count the contents of your cutlery drawer. This way you can quickly identify if any spoons or knives have gone missing that could potentially be used to administer illegal drugs or commit violent crime.

J Dolphin,
Northampton

FINAL round contestants on Jasper Carrott's Golden Balls quiz. Whether you come away with any money is entirely dependent on whether your opponent chooses to 'Split' or 'Steal', so you yourself may as well 'Steal'. That way you double the amount, if any, that you win.

S Hawking,
Cambridge

FARMERS. Get up an hour later in winter, or buy a torch so the rest of us don't have to fart around adjusting our clocks, watches and videos twice a year.

Victorio Angel,
e-mail

AIRLINE pilots. Encourage your passengers to 'get up and move about a bit' while doing 500mph, 30,000 feet above an ocean, but indignantly insist they 'remain seated with their seat-belts fastened' as you dawdle the three miles across the tarmac to the arrival gate at 5mph.

Chris Ash,
e-mail

OBESE Radio 1 breakfast DJs. Why not discuss with your colleagues on air how you intend to spend your £600k salary? Your listener demographic of 16-25 year-old van drivers, warehouse workers and sixth-formers will really appreciate the insight.

Shifty,
e-mail

USED bikini waxing strips make ideal 'scented' doormats for your pet rabbit's hutch.

Paul,
Bedford

SINGLE men. Convince people that you have a girlfriend by standing outside Etam with several bags of shopping, looking at your watch and occasionally glancing inside.

Tubbs,
e-mail

DFS. Avoid the need for a half-price sale every few weeks by not stocking leather suites in orange and lime green.

Dr Albans,
e-mail

LADIES. Cause unnecessary congestion at petrol forecourts by waiting for the pumps on the side nearest your petrol cap, as the 9-foot long hose may not reach round your 5-foot wide hatchback.

I Keir,
e-mail

FELLAS. Keep wives and girlfriends on their toes by murmuring the names of other women whilst pretending to be asleep.

R. J. Gillon, Coventry

THE wire top off a Champagne bottle makes a handy walking frame for lame mice.

Graham Townend, Shipley

DISAPPOINT wasps this summer by smearing cold tea on your ears instead of honey.

T. Shankborne, Coventry

SAVE money on expensive boiled sweets. Give kiddies frozen grapes to suck. They're just as sweet, cheaper to buy and much lower in calories.

Ian Budd, Manchester

NEXT time you fill your tyres with air at the garage, charge the attendant 10p for each breath you take while you're talking to him.

D. Thompson, Wivenhoe

REMOVE all buttons from articles of clothing before you place them in the washing machine. This will prevent the buttons from making a 'clanking' sound when they bang against the glass in the washing machine door.

Mrs I. Graham, Berkshire

BOMB disposal experts' wives. Keep hubby on his toes by packing his lunchbox with plasticine and an old alarm clock.

E. F. Chester-le-Street

SAVE time when crossing a one-way street by only looking in the direction of oncoming traffic.

D. Rogers, Hemel Hempstead

A BICYCLE pump used backwards makes a handy makeshift vacuum cleaner.

T. Elm, Hornchurch, Essex

EXPENSIVE hair gels are a con. Marmalade is a much cheaper alternative, but beware of bees in the summer.

M. Boyle, Surrey

WHEN crossing a one-way street, always look in both directions in case a large, blue furniture removal lorry is reversing the wrong way up the road.

D. Rogers, Hemel Hempstead General Infirmary

GERMAN sex perverts. Rig up a four foot length of garden hose with a shower head on the end, drink ten pints of lager and attach the other end to your knob. Hey presto! Your own, personalised 'Golden Shower'!

A. Bain, Manchester

20

top tips

COUNCIL highway departments. Save money erecting warning signs on dangerous bends. Simply sellotape a bunch of flowers to a nearby lamp post instead.

Adrian Webster, Macclesfield

HIGHWAY agencies. Save warehouse space by putting what is left of your traffic cones in the gaps on the M1.

Pete Harrington, e-mail

FARMERS in Staffordshire. Get up before crow's piss like all other farmers throughout the country do. That way you won't have to do the eight-mile journey to your fields in a tractor at 10mph during the rush hour.

Ex-farmer, e-mail

MOTORISTS. Find out the price of petrol everywhere else by driving to a BP garage and deducting 4p from their displayed price.

Geoff, e-mail

OAPs. Avoid causing annoyance to people at petrol stations by pressing the handle of the nozzle to dispense petrol into your gadgie wagon, rather than staring blankly at the pump wondering why the numbers aren't going round. Either that or get the bus.

Vanessa McGhee, e-mail

BANGING two pistachio nutshells together gives the impression that a very small horse is approaching.

Nigel Austin, e-mail

NIGHT club owners. Improve customer services by employing a man who douses you in perfume and demands money after you've taken a shit. For added effect ensure he shouts "Freshen up?", startling me while I strain.

**J Potts,
e-mail**

WHEN replying to Nigerian lawyers that offer millions in return for a £50.000 finders fee, only send half the money. Keep the rest until you get the paperwork.

**Dr Maldwin Palmer,
e-mail**

HOMEOWNERS. Count your roof-tiles each time you leave the house, so you will know if any of them have been stolen since the last time you counted them.

**Alan Fistula,
Penmaenmawr**

COUCH potatoes. When eating Pringles, conserve energy by removing them from the tube two at a time but only taking half a bite. Hey Presto! You are eating the same amount of Pringles for only half of the arm movements.

**Wooly,
Seaham**

DON'T fork out thousands of pounds on a Jacuzzi-style bath. Make your own by placing a hairdryer in the water. Wear a wetsuit to avoid getting electrocuted.

**Jack Plywood,
Wiltshire**

SALAD lovers. A clever way to store lettuce, cabbage and the like is to individually punch holes in the leaves and place them in a ring binder in the fridge. File cos under 'C', iceberg under 'I' and so on. Simple!

**A Stepney,
Turniptop**

FOOL your friends into thinking you use expensive butter by simply using cheap margarine and ripping holes in the bread.

**Jools B,
e-mail**

KIDS. Threading a piece of string through a ping pong ball and painting it brown is ideal for a fun game of conkers that conforms with the 1974 Health & Safety Act, section 52, paragraph c.

**Grant B Warner,
New Malden**

INTERIM governments. Avoid coalition forces overstaying their welcome by yawning loudly and saying you have an early start in the morning.

**Hamid Karzai,
e-mail**

HAMMER nails through a cricket ball and roll it around in fallen leaves. Hey presto! An Autumn snowball. Cheap and great fun for the kids.

**Matt Greatorex,
e-mail**

BRAZILIANS. Set your watches two hours fast. That way you might arrive wherever you are going on time for once.

**C Penge,
e-mail**

CORDLESS phones make ideal mobile phones for agoraphobics.

Eric,
Morecambe

ANNOY and frustrate SpecSavers staff by wandering up to their counter, squinting your eyes whilst looking up at the price board, and when they ask if they can help you, saying "Big Mac Meal, please."

Richard Karslake,
Oxon

WEATHER presenters. When presenting the forecast, feel free to use both temperature scales for dramatic effect. Use Celsius for cold temperatures (-5°C sounds much colder than 23°F) and Fahrenheit for high temperatures (90°F has much more impact than 32°C)

Chris Stallard,
e-mail

EARN big money by displaying a "How's My Driving?" sign on your car, along with an 0906 number (£1.50 per minute) which you can acquire through BT. Then simply drive around town like a complete arsehole.

Jim,
Lancaster

NORTHERNERS. On hot summer nights go to bed wearing a shower cap full of frozen peas to cool your head. And when you wake up you'll have a tasty mushy pea snack ready for breakfast.

Gary Parslow,
e-mail

ANT & Dec. Have some fun by switching names and seeing if anybody notices or cares.

Dick & Dom,
London

HUSBANDS. Cheer yourself up by watching your wedding video in reverse. You'll love the bit where you give her back the ring, walk back up the aisle, get into a car and fuck off.

Ben Nicol,
Mernda

PENPALS. If you and your penpal should fall out, simply send each other empty envelopes.

Fiona,
e-mail

PEOPLE of normal height and build. Lose about 6 stone before taking a Virgin transatlantic flight. Not only will you now fit into the seat, you might even find it comfortable.

Tina McCormick,
e-mail

BANKS. Offer people loans when they have plenty of money, and refuse them any help when they haven't got a pot to piss in. And waste millions on expensive headed paper.

David Jones,
e-mail

DON'T waste money on a new car with air-conditioning. Simply buy a cut'n'shut that has been in a death crash and let the ghosts keep you cool.

Russ Sheringham

AMATEUR pool players. Appear more skilful than you actually are by grimacing and sounding disappointed after every misplaced shot.

Andrew Fox, e-mail

JULIAN from Anglian Homes. Cover up your phone mouthpiece next time you ask your supervisor what to do, and he replies 'make something up.'

Ted Bundy, e-mail

VOYEURS. Sit on your cock and your hand until they are both numb. Hey presto, it looks and feels like someone else wanking someone else off.

Al F., e-mail

A MIXTURE of human hair, carrot peelings and some congealed fat makes an excellent makeshift plug for any kitchen sink

Simon T Bosun e-mail

DISCARDED PALLETS make ideal 'designer futons' for style-conscious tramps.

Jamaal, e-mail

EBAY sellers. Ensure that everybody looks at your item by writing "L@@K" in the title.

Andy e-mail

RESIDENTS of Stevenage. Save money for Christmas by only buying enough fireworks for bonfire night, instead of enough to last from Halloween till November the fucking 10th.

Brian, Stevenage

THEATRE NURSES. If the surgeon you work with is called Simon, brighten up mundane procedures by refusing to pass any equipment to him until he uses the prefix "Simon Says". Remember even when he shouts "Give me the ligature, this child is DYING!" he's probably just trying to get you out.

Ben Margerison, e-mail

DON'T waste money this Valentine's day buying your wife or girlfriend expensive underwear or chocolates. Simply buy her a pair of edible knickers from Ann Summers and kill two birds with one stone.

Duncan Brown, e-mail

RADIO 5Live listeners. Find out which C-list celebrity will be appearing on the day's talk shows to plug their book or show by watching Breakfast on BBC1 earlier that morning.

Old Biddy, e-mail

LEFT wing celebrities. When offered an OBE or similar gong, don't 'accept it begrudgingly', saying you disagree with system, but it is churlish to turn it down. Simply tell them to fuck off and keep your credibility.

T Thorne, Hexham

CORONATION Street cast members. Don't eat cereal for breakfast as you'll only stab at it moodily with a spoon before pushing it away uneaten. Eat toast and you can wave it about happily while chatting with people.

Arigato Ian Hughes, e-mail

HOUSEWIVES. Here's a splendid way of making your cooking oil go further. Simply leave it on the No.87 bus on the way home from the shops.

**Geraint Crindle,
Liverpool**

EACH month, put a pet mouse down the back of your sofa for a few hours. Hey presto! All the loose biscuit crumbs will be eaten.

**Jason Richardson,
Wallasey**

MAGGOTS make ideal 'sausages' for mice. Cook them over a cigarette lighter using a milk bottle top as a mouse-size mini 'frying pan'.

**B. Newton,
Liverpool**

BIG ISSUE vendors. Have blonde hair and big tits. That way you'll sell more copies.

**G. Rice,
Liverpool**

MOPTOP TIPS

PORNOGRAPHERS. When positioning your centrefolds, try to avoid putting the staples directly over the models' genitals. Not only are they what we've paid to see, it also looks somewhat uncomfortable for the young ladies concerned.

**Isaac Cox,
Liverpool**

CITY gents. Simulate the thrills of ski jumping by leaning forward and placing your umbrella under your arm next time you go down an escalator.

**Matty,
Liverpool**

NEED to measure an alligator but only have a school ruler? Simply measure the distance between its eyes in inches, to give its overall length in feet.

**Jungle John,
Liverpool**

BI-CURIOUS men. Go to a male doctor and complain of rectal bleeding. The resulting erotic anal probe will be a safe way to find out whether gayness is really for you.

**Terry Wilson,
Wallasey**

HALF a Weetabix 'erected' at the end of a mousetrap makes a dignified gravestone for any mice you've killed, and attracts a crowd of mouse 'mourners' to boot!

Ken De Mange,
Leeds

AMERICANS. Save valuable time by not appending the words 'God Bless America' to your every fucking sentence.

John Terry,
Newcastle upon Tyne

LADIES. Avoid parking discrepancies by aiming to park all wonky. There is a good chance you will end up perfectly straight and within the lines.

A Man,
Houseville

GENTLEMEN. Avoid any unnecessary scrotal surgery by removing any genital piercings before using the 'Black Hole' water flume at Butlins, Bognor Regis.

Big Bladder,
e-mail

LADIES. When treating genital thrush, always ensure you use natural bio-yoghurt and not raspberry-flavoured Munch Bunch.

Lee Henman,
e-mail

DON'T bother going to any trouble for loaded, elderly relatives. As their parting shot, they invariably leave the lot to someone who has never lifted a finger to help them.

Cecil Gaybody,
Firkham

HOMELESS people. Take the piss by asking for money 'for a cup of tea' whilst pissed out of your face on Special Brew.

Graham Purple,
e-mail

WASHED-UP celebrities. Earn a bit of extra cash by doing reality TV shows. If that doesn't float your boat, try insurance adverts.

Cardy,
e-mail

JINX thieves by fitting mirrored glass to your house and car. When a thief breaks a window, Hey presto! - seven years' bad luck.

John Hymns,
Macclesfield

GIVE your kitchen a more spacious feel by putting a pile of sprouts at one end and pretending they are far-off cabbages.

Louis Lawson,
Croydon

MAKE your own cherry tomatoes by watering beefsteak tomato plants with bonsai feed.

Mounty Don,
e-mail

PRETEND you are an E4 programme planner by buying DVD box sets of American sitcoms and playing discs at random.

Smiffy,
E-mail

LIGHTEN up worrying trips to the doctors by posing every question with the prefix "Doctor, Doctor".

Christina Martin,
e-mail

SOLDIERS. Invest in a digital camera to avoid all that Court Martial malarkey after a trip to Trueprint.

Phil,
e-mail

ACTRESSES. Next time you do an advert for a constipation remedy, spend some of your fee on a pair of dark sunglasses. That way, when you are in the supermarket you won't have people pointing at you saying "there's the woman with the painful stools."

Gerry Paton,
e-mail

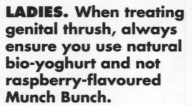

VISITORS to the Argyll Wildlife Park near Inveraray. Avoid paying the entrance fee by simply walking down the lane at the rear of the establishment. Four of the Six animals can clearly be seen from here.

Richard Anke,
e-mail

T-MOBILE customers. Call your phone network and tell them you are moving to another company and ask for your PAC number. They may offer you £30 worth of calls to stay with them (as they did in my case) When this is used up, simply try the same thing again.

Anon,
e-mail

BENT politicians. Conduct interviews in the nude. This will encourage reporters to strip as well, revealing any hidden cameras and tape recorders that could catch you out offering to ask questions for cash or whatever it is you do.

L Aney,
e-mail

CONVINCE your nan that she's going senile by moving the bookmark in her Barbara Cartland novel 10 pages forward while she's not looking.

Adam Riley,
Easington

PEOPLE in lifts. If Bruce Willis gets in wearing a vest and no shoes, exit the lift at the earliest opportunity.

Jason Knight,
e-mail

PEOPLE who don't like eating breakfast. Sit on your cornflakes until they go numb and, hey presto, it feels like someone else is eating your breakfast.

Jason Knight,
Reading

GIVE SPIDERS the nail-biting experience of a real life Indiana Jones adventure by tipping them down a cardboard tube whilst slowly closing the lower end with a playing card. For added excitement roll a Ferrero Rocher down the tube and have a friend insert cocktail sticks through the side at regular intervals.

John Bottom,
e-mail

BASEBALL cap manufacturers. Save the wearer the bother of turning your caps round by putting the peak on the other side.

John Davies,
Carlisle

SUPERMARKETS. Save money on printing by labelling your 'Economy' goods 'Shit' instead.

Cat & Trev,
Newcastle

MEN. When asked by your wife "do you prefer this one... or this one?" simply choose any outfit at random because she won't pay any attention to your decision. It'll just be a complete waste of your fucking time.

J Wipp,
Australia

ONE-ARMED men. If your partner is thinking about getting breast implants, convince her to save money and only get one done.

Sam McCrohan,
Guildford

SPECTACLE wearers. Prepare for any forthcoming conflict by putting crosses of masking tape across the lenses of your glasses.

Clint,
Eastwood

SHOE shop staff. If I ask for a size 9, and all you have left are a size 7 or 12, then for future reference, I would rather not 'give them a try.' Call it intuition or whatever, I just don't think they'd fit.

Dan B,
e-mail

PIGS. Avoid having your head on a dinner table by not eating whole apples.

Neil Polt,
e-mail

KYLIE. Ensure maximum publicity for your next single by shoving a coke bottle up your Jacky Danny, and inviting round the world media.

Rob Salmon,
e-mail

MIDGETS. Draw less attention to your disability by dressing up in children's clothes and passing yourself off as a toddler.

Madeleine McDonald,
Edinburgh

WOULD-BE criminals. Before you commit a crime, get a foretaste of what the world would look like from inside a prison by holding a fork up close to your eye.

R Simple,
e-mail

PROSTITUTES. Helping a client to undress can be sexy, but dressing him afterwards takes him back to childhood when his mother helped him get ready for school.

Tom Brown,
e-mail

LONELY? Simply stand around any city centre smoking a cigarette. Hey presto! A legion of un-washed friends, simply for the cost of a Mayfair.

Daniel Jackson,
Glasgow

GENTLEMEN. Speed up your lovemaking by playing Benny Hill's theme tune Yakkety Sax in the bedroom.

Fisk Kid,
e-mail

SHOES last twice as long if only worn every other day.

Clare Hobley (34E),
Manchester

GERMANS. Don't waste money on expensive, professionally-produced scat movies. Simply set your video to record every athletics meeting involving Paula Radcliffe. Hey Presto! After a couple of years you'll have a scat video library second to none.

Alex W,
Newcastle

RAY MEARS. Lose those extra pounds by not constantly grazing on grass and leaves like some kind of prize-winning cow.

Daniel Green,
e-mail

WANT to feel famous? Simply pop down to your local bistro and sit underneath the 'Specials' board. People will be continually looking in your direction and making comments.

R. Harron, Brixton

TV EXECUTIVES. Looking for a fresh, new idea for top TV Star Danny Wallace? Simply steal one from a book without asking. The authors probably won't mind.

Hampton Framley, e-mail

VIEWERS of Mock the Week. Get the funniest gags from the new series about a month early by simply reading them in the pages of Viz.

Mike Tatham, e-mail

CONVICTS. Avoid unwanted shower room intimacy by choosing instead to take a bath.

Nick Varley, e-mail

SAVE money on tattoos by having a small one done over a muscle, then going to the gym until the muscle gets bigger. Hey presto, a big tattoo for the price of a small one.

Ian Mainy, Bedford

JOHN Fortune. Make your satirical attacks on American corporate greed on the Rory Bremner show carry more weight by appearing in slightly fewer adverts for McDonald's in your spare time.

Roland Butter, Denmark

OFFICE workers. Before shredding paper, write the numbers 1 to 30 across the top. That way you will easily be able to put the paper back together if you accidentally shred something you meant to keep.

T Ketchup, e-mail

GOD. Annoy cyclists by making sure that the wind is blowing in their faces whatever direction they cycle in. For added entertainment, make sure the wind is blowing from behind as people leave the hairdressers.

Grant Warner, New Malden

SAVE money on electric toothbrushes by simply clamping a bottle brush into the chuck of a Black & Decker drill.

S. Grainger, Market Raisin

DON'T buy bright red paint for exterior metalwork from B&Q. Judging by the state of many of their DIY stores, it's really shit.

Steve Lowndes, e-mail

HOMEOWNERS. Don't hesitate to tell the rest of us how much your house has appreciated in value since you bought it. The more frequently you give us updates, the greater will be our delight at your good fortune and our admiration and respect for your financial prescience.

Paul Bradshaw, e-mail

OLD people. Each night, go to sleep in the recovery position, potentially saving paramedics valuable time.

Kev Pick, e-mail

A BLOCK of cheese makes an excellent rubber when writing on bread.

Rev J Foucault, Truro

BIRD Flu could be quickly and easily eradicated by adding a few drops of Lemsip or Daynurse to birdbaths. Obviously, you would have to put Nightnurse in the birdbaths for owls.

Graham Flintoff, Gateshead

DON'T waste money on expensive phone screensavers. Just cut out the one you want from the advert and stick it on your mobile.

S. Potts
e-mail

OLD people. If you feel cold indoors this winter, simply pop outside for ten minutes without a coat. When you go back inside you will really feel the benefit.

Win Dozsthreeone,
e-mail

FITNESS fanatics. When driving to the gym, spend half an hour circling the car park so as to nab a spot as close as possible to the door. That way you won't waste any energy before you embark on your two-hour workout.

Vic C.,
Bedford

NEWSREADERS. Save time in broadcasts by simply reporting when Pete Doherty hasn't been arrested on some drugs charge.

Paul Skinback,
e-mail

TOWN Councils. Reduce litter problems by issuing blind people with pointy sticks.

Rich,
Ilford

DIETERS. Buy only Russian Alphabetti Spaghetti as there are only 22 letters in the Cyrillic alphabet. Just watch the pounds fall off.

Sergei Atkinsov,
e-mail

MAKE striking firefighters leap into action. Set fire to a porn warehouse and see how quick they move.

J Kerin,
Faversham

HEROIN addicts. Instead of getting up at the crack of dawn everyday to go shoplifting to raise money for smack, why not cut out the middle man and simply nick the heroin? Not only will this save time, but it will be much safer as drug dealers' homes don't usually have security guards and CCTV.

Damian Marshall,
e-mail

MOBILE phone users. On trains always choose a seat in the last carriage. Then, when a train enters a tunnel, run as fast as you can towards the front of the train. This will ensure that you are in the tunnel for the shortest possible time and are less likely to miss that all-important call.

Rusty Gronk,
Gateshead

JAZZ SINGERS. Show off your innate rhythmic ability, natural leadership and rat-pack-esque style by clicking your fingers on beats 2 and 4 ever-so-slightly off the beat in front of the bass player. It's a little known fact that as most bass players cannot keep time naturally, the whole thing would fall apart if it weren't for you clicking those fingers, so don't stop whatever you do. You can make it extra fun and unpredictable for the whole rhythm section by occasionally coming back in for the verse in tune and in the right place.

Jazzy2Fives,
e-mail

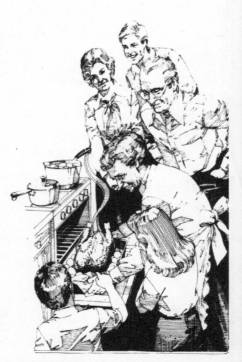

Filter Tips

AVOID the constant price increases in milk by buying all you will need for the rest of the year in January. **Iain Finlayson, e-mail**

Lt Moley Mole, e-mail SAVE electricity by shortening the cables to all your household electric appliances.

DISCARDED heels from gentlemen's shoes make ideal front doors for mouse holes. **Kevin Fluff, e-mail**

Doug, e-mail IMAGINE you are small by sitting in a big tree and pretending it's a bonsai tree. And eating a king-size Mars bar.

Name lost, Sorry PEOPLE called Steven. Save time by calling yourself Steve.

SPOOK owners of cars with tinted windows. Upon seeing one driving past, wink conspiratorially and touch your nose. **Ed Wullbeck, e-mail**

Stavros Curlini, e-mail INCREASE your life expectancy by expecting to live longer than you did beforehand.

PEOPLE called Steve. Save time by calling yourself Ste, (pronounced 'Stee'). **Name lost, Sorry**

31

Pol Pot's Pot Tips

NURSING home staff. Modify a bathtub by attaching roller-skates to the bottom, and next time you give an old man a bath, roll him down a country lane for some *Last of the Summer Wine*-style fun.
MICHAEL EDWARDS, STOCKTON-ON-TEES

OLD PEOPLE. Save having to get a flu jab each year by not queuing outside the Post Office every Tuesday morning in the pouring rain an hour before it opens. They won't run out of money. It's not like the queue outside the butcher's during the war.
SARAH COCKS, E-MAIL

COUNCILLORS. Next time you and your 'personal assistant' travel to somewhere sunny abroad on a fact-finding tour, why not pack some holiday clothes? You won't be inspecting civic amenities all the time, so you may as well take the opportunity to enjoy yourselves. After all, you are giving up your spare time in the service of the public.
TONY PEASE, E-MAIL

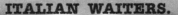

ITALIAN WAITERS. Ensure a warm welcome for your customers by having a good 5-second stare at their wives' tits upon entry, and then another good stare after they have been seated.
LUKE BOUNTY-HUNTER, E-MAIL.

DRINKERS. Towards the end of September, ring companies who specialise in providing personalised wine as corporate Christmas gifts. I have eleven sample bottles on their way to me already.

Jarvis Man,
e-mail

CONVINCE your wife that she's 'followed through' during the night by slipping a chocolate button between the cheeks of her arse as she sleeps.

Ray Devereaux,
Bodmin

OWNERS of mouse circuses. A Toblerone bar makes an ideal bike rack for your display team's motorcycles when they are not in use.

Horst Farqhar,
Warwick

BLIND people. Give yourself at least a chance of seeing something by not wearing heavy dark glasses all the time.

James Smyth,
Hitchin

POWER companies. After a blackout, wait until midnight before turning on the power again. That way, everybody's alarm clocks and videos will be automatically re-set.

Joe Leary,
On fire in Australia

MINIMISE the chance of stepping in canine pavement deposits when it's too dark to see by taking full-length strides with every pace.

Trev,
e-mail

SAVE time when making a cup of tea by pre-heating the water in a saucepan before putting it in the kettle.

Susan Craven,
Leeds

OFFICE partygoers. Impress your colleagues when photocopying your genitals by setting the machine to enlarge by 400%. This works for men only, as the results are less impressive for women.

Eskimo Pope,
e-mail

PAINTBALLERS. Attach a paintbrush onto the end of your gun to use as a 'bayonet' in case you run out of ammo.

H Broom,
e-mail

DON'T buy your sister-in-law a thong for her birthday then expect your wife to be pleased, particularly if you comment on how nice her arse looks in it.

GMK,
e-mail

SAVE HOURS in every working day by hanging the clock upside down at 10.05am. That way, it's 4.35pm and only 25 minutes to home time.

Sod Robin,
Leicester

KEEP a copy of Love Actually or Mrs Doubtfire in your medicine cabinet at home. The last five minutes of these films can induce vomiting if toxic substances have accidentally been swallowed.

T Crone,
Louth

MUMS. Confuse your children by mixing butter with their I Can't Believe It's Not Butter. They won't know what to believe.

Sam McCrohan,
Guildford

BIRDWATCHERS. Save hours sitting around waiting to see which species land on your bird table. Simply mix the food with rat poison and hey presto - dozens of birds laying around the foot of the table for you to inspect and tick off in your book at leisure.

**Stot & Naylor,
Scunthorpe**

GENTLEMEN. Next time you are making love with a lady, cross your eyes. Hey presto! That saucy threesome with identical twins that you've always dreamed of.

**Chunk,
e-mail**

DAYTIME TV viewers. Want to win those phone-in prizes? Follow this easy guide to answering multiple choice questions: (a) is the answer, (b) rhymes with the answer and (c) is in no way the answer.

**Christina Martin,
e-mail**

MARS BAR fans. Buy a Snickers bar and pick out the peanuts. Hey presto, a Mars bar and a handful of peanuts, all for the price of a Snickers.

**Tim Woods,
e-mail**

TEENAGE boys. Stop being mistaken for girls by not having such long hair. Eee! I don't know.

**Ethel Levitt,
London**

TOBACCO manufacturers. Be more positive in your packaging by pointing out that your customers may be able to star in their own TV commercial.

**Tracy Chitty,
Hastings**

CINEMAGOERS. Ensure you get more for your money by only going to see longer films.

**John Shoved,
London**

MATHEMATICIANS. It is always easier to work with smaller numbers, so when adding up big numbers, simply subtract 1 from each figure and then add 2 onto your final number.

**Tim Gibson
e-mail**

CHEFS on Ready, Steady, Cook. Impress the audience by looking away when quickly chopping small vegetables. For added entertainment, set fire to a frying pan every now and then.

**Grant Warner,
New Malden**

MURDERERS. Need to dispose of a body? Simply parcel it up and post it to yourself via DHL. You will never see it again.

**A Langley,
Broadstairs**

POTENTIAL suicidees. Increase your chances by taking more than 10 tablets, locking your front and back doors and not phoning close family friends threatening to 'do something stupid'.

**James Shaw,
e-mail**

PHILANDERERS. Avoid the embarrassment of shouting out the wrong name in bed by only having flings with girls who have the same name as your wife.

Russell Codd, Leeds

MAKE your own inexpensive mints by leaving blobs of toothpaste to dry on a window sill. Use striped toothpaste to make humbugs.

Mark Hughes, Southampton

LADIES. When invited to a Buckingham Palace garden party, go wearing hair rollers, so that the Queen will think you are going somewhere REALLY important afterwards.

Chris Davies, e-mail

CASUALTY DOCTORS. Put the fear of God into any naive male students who have managed to snap their banjo string by whipping out a scalpel and jokily telling them 'Sorry sonny, but the whole thing's got to come off.'

R.A. Urmston, Durham

STREET caricature artists. Avoid telegraphing your sexual fantasies to onlookers by not giving every single young woman huge breasts, a low-cut top and a soft-porn pose. And while you're at it, not all girls have enormous teeth.

Brian Walsh, e-mail

SAVE 20p when using the swimming pool changing rooms at Butlins, Skegness. Lockers 113, 655 and 670 can be locked fully by turning the key without having to deposit a coin beforehand.

C. Frank, Billingham

STATELY home owners. Sprinkle pepper into the helmets of suits of armour so that any intruders who hide in them when being chased will give themselves away by sneezing just after you walk past.

S. Doo, e-mail

VIZ readers. Save money on stamps by not writing in to suggest that a sushi conveyor belt would make an ideal luggage carousel for dwarves.

Hampton Doubleday, Newcastle

TREETOP TITS

TOP CLIPS

CONVINCE your nan that she is losing her marbles by moving the bookmark in her Barbara Cartland novel 10 pages back when she isn't looking.

**M Coxlong,
e-mail**

DON'T waste money on expensive iPods. Simply think of your favourite tune and hum it. If you want to "switch tracks", simply think of another song you like and hum that instead.

**Fish Kid,
e-mail**

SLICING a Battenburg cake lengthways, both vertically and horizontally, makes four handy, long mini sponge cakes (one pair yellow, the other pink).

**R.O. Williams,
e-mail**

WHINGEING southern puffs. Avoid your annual moaning about water shortages and hosepipe bans by filling all your buckets when you get flooded in the winter.

**Peckham,
e-mail**

BUSY mums. Save time making sandwiches by getting your son or daughter to stand on the worktop wearing an ice skate and step onto the middle of each sandwich.

**David Worth,
e-mail**

ACNE scars on your back? Make the most of your disfigurement by having Bryan Adams' face tattooed on one shoulder and Tommy Lee Jones' on the other.

**James Brown,
Edinburgh**

NUDISTS. In cold weather, when you are forced to wear clothes, simply pin a photograph of your cock and balls onto the front of your trousers.

**Al Read,
Halifax**

HOUSEWIVES. Prevent multinational supermarkets from knowing everything about you by simply filling your shopping trolley with things you don't need or want.

**Dan Baker,
e-mail**

MAKE your neighbours think that they live next door to Cliff Richard by stapling a rhino's scrotum to your neck and having a retired vicar move in with you.

Tam Dale,
e-mail

WORM farmers. Double your yield by simply cutting every worm in half. Hey presto! Each half will grow into a new worm.

Laurie,
France

SAUSAGE rolls sewn together side by side make an excellent emergency hat for judges.

Super Ape,
e-mail

ALCOHOL makes an ideal substitute for happiness.

John Hills,
Norwich

MARRIED women. Bored of having sex with the same man again and again? Simply sit on your husband's cock until it goes numb, and hey presto! It feels like someone else is banging you.

Gariath Rubberhead,
e-mail

SEAN Connery. When playing an Egyptian in Highlander or an Irishman in The Untouchables, have a vague stab at the accent for about 5 minutes, then revert back to Scottish.

John Cohen,
e-mail

MORRISONS supermarket in Whitley Bay. Put a nice 10-foot long canopy in the designated smoking area to keep your employees nice and dry whilst they have their fags. Meanwhile, leave the three spaces for bikes open to the elements.

Troy Hurtubise,
Whitley Bay

HORSE riders. Guard against your horse getting fat by giving it Hermesetas instead of sugar lumps.

Tracy Chitty,
Hastings

GOTHS. Save money on expensive black nail polish by striking each fingernail sharply with a toffee hammer.

Ed Anger,
e-mail

TWO sprays of Febreeze makes going down on your missus a much more pleasant experience.

M. Johnson,
Leigh-on-Sea

PARENTS. A small amount of cement added to your child's sandcastle will ensure that his/her hard work is not ruined when the tide comes in.

Corp. Rock & Sgt.
Roll,
e-mail

NORMAL Mars bars make ideal Ice Cream Mars bars for Eskimos.

Burt,
Lancaster

MEN. If you have a bout of wind in a posh restaurant, tell the waiter there are crumbs on your chair. When he comes to remove the crumbs with his little hoover, you can fart to your heart's content.

Ben Jones,
Bristol

McDONALD'S. Make your brown carrier bags green in colour so they blend in with the countryside after they've been thrown out of car windows.

Richard Karslake,
Oxon

BOY racers. Emphasise your prowess as you negotiate the rush-hour traffic by leaning over left or right as you turn the steering wheel.
Mikey Mike, e-mail

VULCANOLOGISTS. If you are ever caught in a volcanic eruption, remember to jump up and down so that your feet are not constantly in the molten lava flow.
Ken Turel, Glasgow

MAKE your postman's day by opening the door as he comes up the path and saying "If there are any bills you can take them back. Ha! Ha! Ha!"
Stu Perry (Postman), Isle of Man

MOVIE-GOERS. If you are late for the start of a film, and think the lights may already be dimmed when you enter the cinema, close one eye about the time you buy your ticket and then open it when you enter the auditorium. Hey presto, you won't be fumbling around in the darkness for the steps or seats.
Brian Derbyshire, Warrington

A PENCIL drawing of a broccoli floret makes an ideal logo for a mouse Conservative Party.
Andy Marsh, E-mail

AN ODOUR-EATER in a jock-strap makes a handy gas mask to protect yourself in the event of a terrorist chemical or biological attack.
R. Charles, London

HOLLYWOOD film makers. Stuck for an idea for a new movie? Simply select the name of an animal or occupation at random and stick the words 'Beverly Hills' in front of it.
Peter Britton, e-mail

HUSBANDS. Tired of sleeping with the same wife? Simply lie on top of her until she goes numb, and Hey Presto! She'll feel like someone else's wife.
Edd Almond, e-mail

RYAN Air passengers. These days they let ALL passengers off the planes, thus eliminating the need to all clamber to the front the second the aircraft lands.
Darren Singleton, e-mail

LEEDS United. Help yourself out of debt by not picking up the Ticket Line phone, and then putting it down again when your supervisor whispers to you to do so.
Angry Matt, Goole

MOVIE-GOERS. Just before your film ends, hold one eye wide open with your thumb and forefinger, so you won't be dazzled by the lights when you leave the cinema.
Brian Derbyshire, Warrington

OLYMPIC commentators. Inform the audience how old the female gymnasts are before they start their routine, thus preventing any illegal thoughts involving their flexibility.
Biliboba Jandouin, e-mail

SIT on your cock till it goes numb. Hey presto! It's just like wanking off somebody else.
Matt, e-mail

Guaranteed 100% Unofficial

TOY TIPS

WEAR a really big cowboy hat to impress the ladies. If your head is too small, remember to cut two eyeholes so you can see.

Tim Burke, e-mail

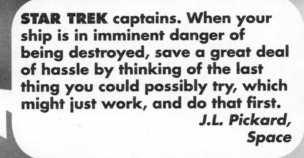

STAR TREK captains. When your ship is in imminent danger of being destroyed, save a great deal of hassle by thinking of the last thing you could possibly try, which might just work, and do that first.

J.L. Pickard, Space

RECENTLY defunct and apparently worthless European coins still work as legal tender for buskers, beggars, the honesty box in WHSmith and old ladies collecting for charities. Especially the RNIB.

Jamie Groves e-mail

HOMEOWNERS. When going upstairs, walk up two and then back one. That way your neighbours will think you have more stairs than them.

Hiapop, e-mail

GARDENERS. Wrap seedling potatoes in a wire mesh before planting. Hey, presto! Ready-cut chips at harvest time.

Basil Pigsfanny, Nottingham

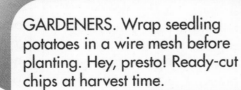

Top Trips

BEFORE brushing your teeth, eat something sweet, such as a piece of chocolate. That way you can be sure of getting good value for the toothpaste that you use.
John Twomey, Kilburn

SUBMARINE designers. Why not put any water pipes on the outside of the sub? That way, if they burst, there is no harm done.
Jim Hogan, e-mail

SCRABBLE PLAYERS. If you have a Q and a U, try to use the Q for words like 'Qi' or 'Qat'. This will free up the U for words like 'Bum', 'Mum' etc.
Stu, e-mail

IMPOTENT men. Don't waste money on expensive drugs like Viagra off the internet. Just let your wife think you don't fancy her.
A Davis, e-mail

A MALT loaf is just the right size and colour to sculpt a convincing pair of decent-sized human turds. Don't forget to taper one end.
Matt Webb, e-mail

HOUSEHOLDERS. Store yellow crayons, broken pencils, dried up biros and highlighters somewhere handy. I keep mine in a jar by the telephone.
Mikey, e-mail

BARGAIN sofa hunters. If you missed the DFS December Sale, Double Discount Boxing Day Sale, January Clearance Sale and the February End of Winter Sale, don't worry - the Spring Sale starts in March.
Hanks Martin, Somewhere

QUEENS. If a large jewel falls out of one's sceptre, it can easily replaced with a pear drop of the same colour, from which one has sucked the sugar coating.
HM Queen Elizabeth II, Windsor

CYCLISTS. Avoid getting a sore arse by simply placing a naan bread over your saddle. This will comfort your ride and when you return home, hey presto! A warm snack.
Chris Pearson, Southampton

RAPPERS. Avoid having to say "know what I'm sayin'?" all the time by actually speaking clearly in the first place.
J Calabas, e-mail

SAVE money on expensive air fresheners by sticking lavender up your arse. Then every time you fart, a burst of soothing fragrance is released into your home.
M Hinge, e-mail

EXECUTIVES. Don't get stressed wasting money on anti-stress toys. Simply fill a condom with diarrhoea and tie a knot in the end. Hey presto! Your own anti-stress toy to squeeze all day long.
Laurence Lennin, e-mail

FOOTBALL commentators. When a player is mouthing off at the referee, make people think you are cleverer than you actually are by insisting that he is 'remonstrating' rather than arguing.
R Clemence, e-mail

SHOE bombers. Increase your payload by becoming a clown.
Mark Johnson, e-mail

SKATEBOARDERS. Stop your trousers from falling halfway down your arse by wearing a strip of perforated leather with a buckle around your waist.
Lee Christopher, e-mail

GENTLEMEN. I find a copy of Razzle Readers' Wives Special makes obeying that tricky 10th commandment about not coveting thy neighbour's wife that bit easier.
Brendan Stitch, e-mail

USERS of premium rate sex lines. Save hundreds of pounds by phoning the Samaritans and threatening to kill yourself unless they talk to you in a sexually-explicit manner.
Rabbi Tableknife, Middlesbrough

LADIES! Putting your mouth and chin inside a pint glass and sucking hard for three minutes is an excellent way to give yourself a "Fred Flintstone" five o'clock shadow.
Michelle Armsponder, Port Sunlight

STUDENTS. Avoid spending a chunk of your student loan on expensive 'out-of-bed-look' hair gels by simply getting out of bed.
Chris Preston, Manchester

HOMELESS people. Lighten your load by not buying a dog.
Ryan, e-mail

KEEN on owning a hamster? Simply urinate in the corner of your room and make a nick in the end of your finger with a kitchen knife every couple of weeks for 18 months.
Jon, e-mail

BREAD knives can also be used to cut cheese.
Benjamin Gardner, e-mail

RABBIS. Get with the times by dressing up like chart teen sensations The Jonas Brothers instead of 80s rockers ZZ Top.
Jofus O'Hooligan, e-mail

THE NIGHT after eating a real ring-stinger of a curry, put a dozen or so ice cubes down the bog. The splashback caused when you have a shit will cool and soothe your burning ringpiece.
Dan, Cambridge

ENJOY indoor snorkeling by filling a bath with water, then removing the plug quickly, putting your mouth over it and breathing through the overflow.
A. Mawdsley, e-mail

SEX offenders with a taste for elderly ladies. Lure your victims into your car with the promise of medicine and slippers.
D. Smith, e-mail

BEE keepers. Avoid getting stung by bees by buying honey in a health food shop and getting stung there instead.
Gary D, e-mail

SAVE money on Red Nose Day by simply using half the wax covering from a tasty Babybel cheese. Save your friends money too by giving them the other half.
J Routlidge, e-mail

GCSE Students. Don't worry if you fail your Religious Education exam. Simply ignore the result and assign yourself an A-grade, telling anyone who objects that it is your solemn belief that you passed.

Christina Martin,
e-mail

GENTS. Save yourself embarrassment on washday. Place a strip of 1-inch wide sellotape in the gusset of your underpants every morning. This can simply be wiped clean after any unfortunate accidents.

Kenny,
Fife

GAMBLERS. Convince fellow punters that you have some inside knowledge by simply cheering every race winner and then counting a wad of cash in your pocket.

Nick Smith,
Leeds

AIR TRAVELLERS. Make your suitcase easy to spot at the luggage carousel by fastening an extremely long-lasting sparkler to it and lighting it before you hand it over at the check-in desk.

Peregrine Fadge,
Jedburgh

SUPERMARKETS. Help promote healthy living by putting your cakes, ice creams, pies etc., in aisles that are too narrow for fatties to fit through.

Serena Keough,
e-mail

JOURNALISTS for local TV stations. Fool viewers into thinking you have been sent abroad by waiting a few seconds before answering questions the presenter asks you.

Douglas Castle,
Beecormack

TAME budgies and parrots easily by replacing their grit with iron filings. By holding a large magnet, they will sit happily on your hand for hours.

Debbie Forster,
e-mail

RECREATE the smell of farts by opening a pack of Iceland's diced chicken.

Grant Warner,
New Malden

RECREATE the feeling of time travel by falling asleep on the train and awakening on arrival at your destination. Hey presto, you've arrived in the future!

Geoff Wilson,
Nottingham

BARE patches on your lawn? Simply stop mowing a patch at the side and let it grow to a significant length. Then, with a rake, sweep it over the bare patch like Sir Bobby Charlton and TV's Robert Robinson do, to create a realistic look of healthy growth.

Tycho Andrews,
Fulham

RHUBARB steeped in bleach makes a fantastic substitute for celery.

Tova Dolin,
e-mail

IF A member of your family suffers with Parkinson's disease, increase their self esteem and sense of worth by making sure they are the first to handle a new bottle of sauce at mealtimes.

D. Lee,
e-mail

ALZHEIMER'S sufferers make perfect April Fool's Day prank victims all year round.

Adam Wigglesworth,
e-mail

GIVE yourself the impression of being 'high' by lying down in a really hot bath whilst smoking a fag, then standing up as if the Queen had just walked in.
Glenn Wild, Rotherham

CRIMINALS. Keep a handkerchief in your back pocket. When the police put handcuffs on you, simply cover your hands with the handkerchief for a few seconds. When you remove it, the cuffs will be unlocked and off. I have seen magicians do this many times and it always works.
Pat Roig, New Orleans

KEEP confusing Sonny and Cher with Sunnis and Shias? Just remember that the former two are an American husband and wife pop duo, the latter are denominations of Islam who have been warring since the death of the prophet Mohammed over which group has the rightful claim to his succession. Simple.
Alan Cardboard, e-mail

DEVOUT CATHOLICS. If the Lord has not yet made Himself visible, perhaps you are looking in the wrong place. Try paying more attention to the flaking paint on your walls, the rust on your frying pan or the mouldy stains on your carpet as these are the sort of places where He usually turns up.
Jon Sangham, West Ho

PARENTS of identical twins. Save money on costly school photographs by simply having one of your children snapped, then photocopying the resultant print. Repeatedly remark to visitors how incredibly similar your children are in order to disguise your deception.
Stewart Cowley, e-mail

GIRLFRIENDS. Increase your chances of getting the fairytale wedding you've always dreamed of by pretending to share your partner's love of frequent, adventurous sexual activity. A week or so after the wedding, you can safely revert back to your prudish, uninterested self again while you pore over the photos and videos of your big day.
B Tait, Fife

HEALTH SERVICE managers. Save millions by replacing the costly NHS Direct service with a simple recorded message that says, "It's probably OK, but if it doesn't start getting better, pop along to Accident and Emergency."
Martin W., London

ATTENTION shandy drinkers. I've found that mixing Kaliber and Hooch makes a fantastic 'reverse shandy'.
Big Heed, Maidenhead

TOP SKIPS

NEW BIKERS. When the driver of a lorry flashes you out and you want to show your appreciation, just nod your head. Under no circumstances wave at him with your right hand. This hand controls the throttle. Lifting this hand OFF the throttle makes the bike come to an abrupt stop. This action will not only cause you to violently lurch forward and make you smack your face on your own headlamp, it will also brighten the day of the lorry driver who will be sat in his cab pissing himself laughing.

John Mason, e-mail

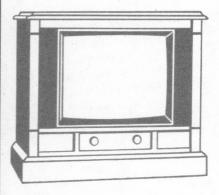

LAD MAG cover photographers. When photographing cover girls pulling their knickers down, wait an extra second after they place their thumbs in the waistband before taking the picture. That way we might actually see something interesting.

Cameron Morley, e-mail

NEWSAGENTS. Keep some change in your till. It's highly likely your customers won't always have the exact money, and that way you won't have to give them a hard time just for buying a paper with a £5 note.

Jimmy James, e-mail

CITY Link. Tell your customers that when the driver ticks "We'll try again the next day", he actually meant to tick the "Come and pick your package up from the depot" box. When your customer points out that the driver gave a specific time for the delivery, claim that your local branch "No longer re-delivers the next day for H-grade packages", whilst scribbling an 'H' on the package with a permanent marker when you think he can't see.

Gary, Eltham

LADY Drivers. Save money by ordering your shopping online and having it delivered. It only costs a fiver, which is a lot less than all the petrol you use trying to park your tiny car in a great big space whilst bringing the whole supermarket car park to a fucking halt every Saturday.

V. Higham, E-mail

GENTS. When coming out of a florist's shop, always punch the first person that you see to ensure that no one thinks you are gay.

Guy A. Bell, Plymouth

HOME Office officials. Save the expense of sending David Blunkett on pricey trips to international conferences in South East Asia. Simply pop him in a flight simulator for eight hours, then sit him down in a sauna for two weeks feeding him chop suey-flavoured Pot Noodles.

Iain McKie, London

EMPLOYERS. Avoid hiring unlucky people by immediately tossing half the CVs into the bin.

Johnny the E., e-mail

TRAMPS. Watch Ray Mears' World of Survival in Dixons' window to open your eyes to a whole host of natural foodstuffs.

Daniel Green, e-mail

IAN HISLOP. Win Have I Got News for You by being funnier than Paul Merton and looking less like Penfold from Dangermouse.

Dave Downes, Nottingham

DEATH ROW prisoners. Increase your life span by a few days by having your last meal delivered from Pizza Hut.

Grant B. Warner,
New Malden

GUYS. Save wasted trips to the swimming baths by ringing them up to ask if there is any bikini-clad talent in the pool before you set off.

David Wells,
Billericay

GENTLEMEN. Upon leaving your favourite adult store into a busy street, affect an expression of utter shock, just in case.

John Mitchell,
e-mail

WORRIED that your teeth will be stained after a heavy night drinking red wine? Simply drink a bottle of white wine before going to bed to remove the stains.

Nick Pettigrew,
London

HOTELIERS. Save money on expensive promotions. Simply christen your beautiful daughter with the name of your hotel, film her having sex, and release the footage on the internet. Hey presto - instant worldwide advertising!

P. Ming,
Paris

NEW ZEALAND tax inspectors. Save time by scrapping the section on the IR3 form asking people to declare 'income from illegal enterprises' as it is unlikely to elicit a great deal of response.

M. Barrymore,
New Zealand

PLACE an ice-cream tub in the basin to catch any excess water while washing hands. You'll quickly collect enough to flush the loo.

Alice Ridden,
E Sussex

PETER KAY fans. Save money on DVDs and tour tickets by going to Bury market instead where you can hear lots of references to parkin, Chorley cakes and Eccles cakes which you all seem to find so fucking hilarious.

Ted Bartlett,
e-mail

TEACHERS. Avoid fancying 15-year-old girls in your charge by picturing them engaged in much younger activities, such as sucking large lollipops or frolicking naked in a paddling pool.

Bellester Smith,
e-mail

CHOCOLATE lovers. Beat the credit crunch by buying two-fingered Kit-Kats instead of four, snapping them in two lengthways and rejoining the two pieces side by side.

Mr Tomo,
e-mail

PARENTS. Avoid throwing the baby out with the bath water by using an ordinary kitchen sieve or some chicken wire loosely attached to the bath.

Mrs Peggy Sarsons,
Oldham

CINEMA goers. Please have consideration for pirate DVD viewers by having a piss before the film starts.

Paul Collins,
e-mail

FELLAS. Caress your girlfriend's back and arms occasionally to give the impression that you are not just interested in her sexual parts.

James Broom,
Paris

MOBILE party DJs. Having trouble getting nervous guests up and dancing? Try petulantly demanding "What's wrong with you?", and calling them all "boring". That should do the trick.

Mark Glover,
Coventry

RESTLESS SOULS. Speed up lengthy ouija board sittings by using text-speak abbreviations.

Mrs D Stokes,
Limbo

CITY Link couriers. The address on the side of the carton holds many gems of information, for example, the name of the town as well as the street. Because, believe it or not, there is more than one Royal Avenue in the country.

Adrian,
Royal Avenue, UK

TV NEWS reporters. Intersperse your interviews with footage of yourself nodding like a twat. This will help viewers appreciate that what's being said is important and correct.

A Quinn,
London

BUSINESSMEN. Fill those awkward silences in the lift by telling people made-up stories about your adventures as a sailor.

C Martin,
e-mail

GARETH Gates. Avoid embarrassing bouts of stuttering by simply singing your replies to questions.

Matt Douse,
Beverley

DUTCH masters. Try a little more light in your paintings. It's often difficult to see what's happening in the corners.

Peter Drobinski,
e-mail

OLD people. Attach a sweeping brush to the front of your mobility trolley. Now, instead of being a menace on the pavements, you can provide a valuable service to your community.

Ben Reeves,
Hove

ROSH HASHANAH

YOM KIPPUR

HOLLYWOOD leading men. When chasing muggers in a London park at 4.00am, avoid tripping over your little dog by carrying it in a shoulder bag.

T Nunn,
Kennington

CONTESTANTS on Bullseye. Give your address as the Moon. That way, if you lose, your 'bus fare home' will amount to several million pounds.

Steve Chiltern,
e-mail

OIL companies. Avoid having the general public pointing the global warming finger at you by putting some pictures of trees and flowers on your websites and adverts.

Will Neale,
e-mail

DRIVERS. When the salesgirl in your local petrol station holds your banknote up to the light, simply wink at her, laughingly telling her "the ink's still wet!" Trust me, she won't have heard this one before, and you might even get a shag.

Rosemary,
Billericay

EX Blue Peter presenters. Start crying on telly when questioned about the death of your dog. People will never suspect that you used to give him a good hiding with his lead as I once saw you do in Halifax in 1978.

Fat Al White,
Wrenthorpe

BIG TOP TIPS

PRETEND

TO BE A TINY PERSON BY POURING ALL THE CRISPS FROM A MULTI-PACK BAG INTO THE BIG BAG THEY CAME IN, AND EATING THEM OUT OF THAT.

MR. ALASTAIR BAVERSTOCK, E-MAIL

 ## TIME TEAM

PRODUCERS - GET MORE DONE IN THE THREE DAY TIME LIMIT BY GETTING BALDRICK AND THAT LAZY FUCKER WITH THE WISPY WHITE HAIR AND STRIPY JUMPER TO DO SOME FUCKING WORK

MATTY
EMAIL

EXHIBITIONISTS

Strain your eyes until they go numb before masturbating, then it will feel like someone else is watching you.

Mr. John Budd,
Reading

NUDISTS

Keep your testicles cosy and warm during cold snaps by popping your scrotum into a 'string vest' made from one of those net bags you get with washing tablets.

Mr. Al Read,
Halifax

FOOL

potential car thieves into thinking there is a large dog in your parked vehicle by leaving the windows slightly open.

 Mr. George Thrakes,
Chester-le-Street

QUEENS

Don't throw away old crowns. They make excellent cosies for Ming Dynasty teapots.

HM Queen Elizabeth II,
Windsor

DIABOLISTS. For the full effect when photographing

Satan, make sure to switch off your camera's red-eye reduction feature.

 Mr. Paul Bradshaw,
e-mail

DRUG dealers. Turn your users into fun aquariums by cutting your gear with sea monkeys.

Pandeviant, e-mail

FOOL your boss into thinking that your alarm clock is broken by continually turning up late for work in the morning.

Kris Mortimer, e-mail

NON-SMOKERS. Convince everyone that you are a sixty-a-day man by smearing the fingers of your right hand with iodine.

S MacRat, e-mail

CHERYL from London. Stop your husband from shagging the redhead down the Coach and Horses by occasionally sucking his dick, you frigid cow.

T. Moss, London

WOMEN. Why take two bottles into the shower when you can take about a dozen, cluttering up the shelf so there is no room for the single bottle of all over shampoo that we men seem to be able to manage perfectly well with? For fuck's sake.

Iain Purdie, Bradford

WIFE of Jacko out of Brush Strokes. Burst into the bathroom next time you think your husband is cleaning. You will probably catch him boasting to a hidden camera about how he has pulled the wool over your eyes and is off on a golfing holiday with his mates. Then you can divorce him and marry a less nondescript actor, like Eric out of Lovejoy.

Ben Brundell, Halifax

CONTESTANTS on Wife Swap. Try not to be so surprised at how different the other family is. That is, and always has been, the format of the show.

Martin Christiansen, e-mail

BRITISH Airways. Next time you run out of breakfasts mid-way through serving a Montreal to Heathrow flight, why not just admit it, instead of mumbling stuff about "we're just waiting to find something" before serving half the plane three dry bread rolls and a fucking bar of chocolate?

A. Rugby, Newcastle

RADIO 5Live's Victoria Derbyshire. Instead of cutting racist callers off half way through their diatribe, simply don't bate them to call your poxy phone-in show in the first place by asking loaded questions like "What would YOU do about the immigrants?"

J. Thorn, Hexham

CONSTIPATION sufferers. Get your GP to prescribe antidepressants, as they loosen you up like nobody's business. Though how being stuck on the toilet all day dribbling yellow treacle out of my arse is meant to cheer me up I have no idea.

S. Monkey, e-mail

SHOE manufacturers. Stop your shoes giving people blisters by making them out of plasters.

S Pigeon, e-mail

ABSENT-MINDED people. Don't waste money on post-it notes. Simply find an elephant that lives locally and tell them whatever it is you need remembering.

C. Martin,
e-mail

MARKS & Spencer. Save on your printing costs by only sending blokes the lingerie section of your catalogue.

S Mencer,
E-mail

BRA-LESS feminists. Support your sagging breasts by pretending you have a broken arm and wearing a sling. Simply shorten the sling until your tits reach a socially-acceptable level.

S. Ballard,
e-mail

CLIMATE change activists. Feel less guilty about travelling by plane by breathing more shallowly whilst on holiday.

The Beed,
Dudley

A USED condom filled with water and left on a radiator makes an ideal and inexpensive lava lamp.

T. Hogan,
e-mail

SWISS people. Claim neutrality during the next world war so that you can hoard Nazi loot and pilfer Jewish gold.

Barney Waygood,
Edinburgh

VIRGIN Trains. Why not re-name the 16:58 Preston to Euston train the 17:05 because that's the fucking time it turns up every day?

Denis Wilkinson,
e-mail

BUYING chain or wire at B&Q? Cut off the length you want and abandon it elsewhere in the store. Next day, buy it from the reduced bucket for half price.

Edd Hillman,
e-mail

RECREATE the feeling of being a five-year-old on your first day at school by going to your doctor's surgery and having a conversation with the receptionist.

Glen Stone,
e-mail

WANKERS. Attach a pedometer to your wrist and measure the calories you burn. Then you can proudly tell your wife how much exercise you have done.

Andrew Tatham,
e-mail

BOYS. Two pieces of used chewing gum stuck together make an ideal brain when lobotomising your action man.

Jeremy Rubbish,
e-mail

DEPRESSED people. Instead of attempting suicide as a 'cry for help', simply shout "Help!", thus saving money on paracetamol, etc.

Stephen McGrath,
e-mail

DURING winter, put pop tarts on your radiators so you can have a warm snack throughout the day whilst saving electricity on your toaster.

Dave Oxendale,
York

HOME decorators. Use a roller in each hand and halve your painting time.

B&Q,
Swallwell

CINEMA builders. Don't bother installing a front row of seats, nobody ever uses them. Simply start with the second row.

Dave Stuttard,
Warrington

HARDCORE Hispanic gangsters from South Central L.A. Save money on expensive hairnets by using the satsuma bags from Aldi in Redcar.

Chat Mon Yat,
e-mail

A BEERMAT cut diagonally in half and fastened together with lengths of string makes an ideal bra for Tara Palmer-Tompkinson.

Rob Jackson,
Tinshill

TO MAKE a pot of supermarket coleslaw go further, simply grate a carrot, some cabbage and an onion into the tub, then add some mayonnaise.

S.A.,
Derby

RE-USABLE canvas shopping bags make an excellent receptacle to store all the bags you are left with after trips to the supermarket.

Milton Banana,
e-mail

SPECS wearers. Save money on alcohol by simply drinking half as much, then taking your glasses off for the same pissed-up effect.

Rich,
e-mail

HEIRS to the throne. Save money by giving your dead mother's engagement ring to your fiancée, and pretending it's 'romantic'.

Andy Mansh,
e-mail

SAVE money on your water bill. Every time you flush the toilet, piss into the cistern. It all goes down the same way and you'll save approximately £1.56 over a lifetime.

Albert Shortfish,
West Midlands

BBC Economics correspondents. Plot a graph of the monthly change in average house prices as opposed to the prices themselves. That way, you will get an alarming and headline-grabbing 'downward line' even when house prices are still going up.

Torbjorn Earpiece,
Luton

CITY Link Couriers. When delivering parcels to an address you are unfamiliar with, why not check on your GPS system. This will save you the hassle of telling your boss you tried to deliver it but there was nobody in. It would also save the poor sod who had waited in all day from taking another day off work.

Justin Credible,
e-mail

DAVINA McCall. Disguise your lack of TV presenting ability by gurning excessively at any nearby camera. Nobody will notice a thing.

Podge,
e-mail

PHOTOGRAPHERS. Confuse darkroom technicians by taking pictures of your negatives and developing positive negatives.

Harry Partridge,
e-mail

LADIES. Make your own industrial floor polisher by sliding a pair of your hubbie's towelling socks onto the blades of a Flymo.

Matt Rundle,
e-mail

POSTMEN. Increase your chances of receiving a Christmas tip from grateful customers by not being such a fucking misery for the other 51 weeks of the year.

Warwick Sloss,
Bristol

GUN jumpers. Avoid premature ejaculation during intercourse by offloading during foreplay.

Y.I. Never,
e-mail

TODD'S TIPS

POTATOES
wrapped in tin-foil
and kept in a cupboard
become a welcome
consolation snack if your
house burns down.
Barry Chocolate,
e-mail

AT SUPERMARKET
checkouts, a Toblerone
box makes an ideal
'Next Customer Please' sign
for dyslexic shoppers.
M. Axell,
Middlesbrough

CELERY with a
bit of jam on makes
an excellent rhubarb
substitute.
Tova Dolin,
e-mail

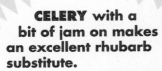

MINIMISE
the risk of breaking
your arm by avoiding
swans wherever possible.
H. Lloyd,
Billingham

KEEP an
empty bottle of milk
in your fridge in case
someone wants black
coffee or even tea.
Richard Hawkins,
e-mail

LADIES. Prevent sexist workmen from shouting "Get yer tits out!" by having them permanently on display.

Hoolmes,
e-mail

ORDINARY people. Make yourselves feel more important by carrying a bugle everywhere you go and sounding it before you enter.

L Luton,
Wolverhampton

WANKERS. Save yourself a great deal of embarrassment by checking that none of your housemates has come home from work sick and is sleeping in their room before you put a porn vid on in the living room with the volume on high.

Lachlan Barker,
e-mail

MAKE your new neighbours immediately regret moving into their new home by introducing yourself as a "senior resident of the street" and telling them that "everyone round here likes things just the way they are".

Guy,
Nottingham

MEN. Attract loads of gorgeous women in the most remote locations by simply releasing a foul-smelling fart. They will appear as if by magic at this inopportune time.

Steve Morris,
Cheshire

SAVE money on expensive helicopter rides by walking up Snowdon in December wearing jeans, trainers and a t-shirt.

May Hinge,
e-mail

SPAGHETTI Bolognese makes great intestines for a badly wounded Action Man

Dean Hale,
e-mail

INITIAL City Link. Instead of the slogan you have painted on the sides of your lorries - "Your reputation in a box? We guarantee it...every time!" why not use the wording of clause 4.5 of your Standard Trading Conditions - "Whilst the Company shall use its reasonable endeavours to comply with any estimate given by the Company to the Customer, any delivery time (including date) given by or on behalf of the Company shall be an estimate only, time shall not be of the essence and shall not be binding upon the Company which shall be under no liability whatsoever, except as provided for in Clause 17, for failure to secure delivery of any Goods by any date or time howsoever caused," which more accurately reflects your approach to the punctual delivery of urgent packages.

U. Kirby,
Follingsby Park

FEMALE newsreaders. Tell viewers at the start of each bulletin whether or not you are wearing a bra, then we won't waste half an hour trying to figure it out for ourselves.

Chris,
e-mail

HORSE whisperers. Speak louder. This will enable the animals to hear you more clearly, thus speeding up training times.

Nameworth Lostbridge,
Sorryhampton

LIAM Gallagher. When singing, lower the microphone a bit so that it's in front of your mouth. This will prevent any unnecessary neck strain. How you could stop being a cunt, though, is beyond me, I'm afraid.

Gary Parslow,
e-mail

McDONALD'S. Save money on glass by not building a 'window number 1' in your drive-throughs as there is invariably never anybody there.

M. B. Lloyd,
Fawdon

LADIES. A 'guide bat' tethered to your finger with a short piece of string is the perfect way to avoid trees and horses in the dark.

G. Lineker,
e-mail

AMERICAN High School teachers. Increase your efficiency by announcing which chapters to read from the textbook for next class some time before that fucking annoying bell rings.

Justin Deegan,
e-mail

IF you fall over backwards in the street, avoid embarrassment by pretending that you are re-creating Charlie George's 1971 FA Cup goal celebration for Arsenal against Liverpool.

Jarty McBangkok,
e-mail

ANARCHISTS. When smashing the state, take care not to burn down your dole office.

Charles Palmer,
e-mail

WHEN buying a new bin, always buy two in case one isn't very good and has to be thrown away. That way you will always have something to put it in.

Paul Smeenis,
e-mail

LADIES. Leaving your curtains open when undressing will ensure that, in the event of any unfortunate accident, anyone watching you through binoculars can quickly summon help.

Rab Saughton,
e-mail

WOMEN travel writers. Get paid a fortune to travel somewhere wonderful and exotic and then submit the usual article about about how useful a sarong is.

Dave Stuttard,
e-mail

DRUNKEN ladies. When applying your 'Always' sanitary pad with wings, always make sure you position the pad with the sticky side down.

Margaret,
St Helens

A POST-IT note stuck beneath the nose is an ideal deterrent to lip-readers.

Bryn Littleton,
Chester-le-Street

CONVINCE your friends that you play the trombone by standing behind a screen and farting into a watering can.

Peter Hall,
e-mail

FOREIGNERS. Improve your English swearword vocabulary by dawdling aimlessly with your friends in front of the entrance to Oxford Circus tube station at 5.30pm every afternoon. Advanced linguists might like to try zig-zagging down the steps at a snail's pace while texting everyone back home.

Mark Glover,
Coventry

CONSTIPATED driving instructors. Alleviate your discomfort by disconnecting the dual controls on the car when instructing a new pupil. If a stronger laxative effect is required, do the same thing but with a female learner.

Stanley Etherington,
e-mail

PLACING your penis in the bottom of your girlfriend's popcorn box will give her a real shock at the cinema. Especially if you're at home watching football at the time.

Michael Edwards,
Stockton-on-Tees

WHEEL manufacturers. Take a tip from the marketing techniques of makers of men's razors and release a new model every year claiming to be 'the roundest wheel yet.'

Ash Bracey,
e-mail

TOWN planners. Confuse commuters and pensioners by calling new developments 'Sorry this bus is not in service'.

Martin Rafferty,
Nottingham

CRYSTAL TIPS AND ALEISTER

SAVE money on toilet paper by wiping your arse on a flannel. This can be re-used once your wife or girlfriend has washed it.
Barry D.,
e-mail

AMATEUR astronomers. Avoid total blindness by viewing the sun through a telescope rather than binoculars.
Simon Hollingworth,
Norwich

MAKE delayed train journeys fly for everyone by tutting and sighing as much as you can down the closest person's earhole.
Keren Kehoe,
e-mail

DON'T waste your money on a penis enlarger. Simply cut your pubic hair very short. I've done it and it looks great.
Shabby Mack,
e-mail

SERIAL killers. Make amends to the families of your murder victims by sending them a jar of Quality Street.
Craig Sullivan,
Leeds

A GUINEA pig makes an ideal paint roller for your next home make over. Use a mouse for areas that need finer detail.
Ian Vince,
Falmouth

ANGLERS. Save money on expensive 20-foot-long fishing rods by buying a 6-foot rod and sitting on the opposite bank of the canal.
P. Watkinson,
e-mail

TOP PITS

DEAL or No Deal producers: Save money on packaging by using simple envelopes to reveal the cash amounts, rather than using a whole box of which only the underside of the lid is used.

Lee Howse, Catford

MORRISSEY fans. If you're going to throw a plastic water bottle at Morrissey, do it towards the end of his encore rather than halfway through the second song of the evening. That way, you should get slightly better value for your £45 ticket.

S Baldwin, Uttoxeter

AIR guitar players. Become air ukulele players by shortening the distance between your hands. For that added Formby feeling, substitute head moshing with a cheeky smile and the occasional wink.

Matt Douse, Beverley

OLD people. Next time you start a conversation with the words "Of course, it goes without saying…" you can then simply shut up, because whatever you were about to say obviously goes without saying.

Adrian Horsman, Banbridge, Co. Down

FAT CHEMISTRY teachers. Lose weight by drinking neat liquid helium. After quaffing a cup of the icy refreshment, stand on the scales on tippy toes and hey presto! The pounds will simply have dropped off.

Lemon Circus, North Tees

STUDENTS. When visiting the cinema ensure that a long queue has formed behind you and that the cashier has already issued a full price ticket before you ask for a student discount.

A Cinema Manager, Berkshire

PS. Oh, and while you're at it, don't forget to pay with a fucking credit card.

MONKS. Conduct a life of celibacy and emotional solitude without joining a monastery by simply living with my wife. It's more comfortable and you'll be able to watch TV and use the internet.

Not-So-Private Ryan, e-mail

UNDERTAKERS. Put a flashing yellow light on the top hat of the man walking in front of the hearse to warn other road users of the slow procession of cars.

Campbell Moore, e-mail

SMOKERS. "Every cigarette you smoke takes 10 seconds off your life", health experts say. To combat this, at the end of every day work out how many seconds you have 'lost', and simply go to bed that much later, or wake up that much earlier the next morning. Hey presto! your lost time is returned.

James Powell-Brett, e-mail

SHOE Express customers. Throw your purchases away and wear the boxes instead. They'll be harder-wearing, more stylish and better fitting.

Steph Jackson, Newcastle

WALLPAPER manufacturers. Measure the height of a average-sized living room, add 3 inches to the top and bottom and then multiply by 4. Then subtract 2 feet just to ensure the bastards can't get four lengths from each roll.

Tom Scott, e-mail

CHILEAN miners. Take a large range of pornography and crossword puzzles to work with you, just in case.

Jason Richardson, e-mail

SAVE money on expensive surround-sound home cinema systems by only watching films when the appropriate noises are going on outside, e.g. watch horror movies when there is a storm on, or cowboy films whilst local drug gangs are fighting it out in the street.

Andy Mansh,
Cheltenham

COMEDY fans. If you're going to a Frankie Boyle show, don't forget to take a kazoo along and toot it just before each punchline.

Orbis McCeremony,
London

ROOFERS. Try going up on the roof to inspect it, rather than standing at ground level next to me saying "it needs a lot of work done to it."

Mr Slater,
e-mail

OLD people. Ensure a good fight at your wake by leaving a valuable antique in your will to a distant relative, whilst promising it to a closer relative verbally before you die.

T. Poldark,
Cornwall

ORIGAMI ENTHUSIASTS. Save money on expensive brown paper by simply folding Happy Shopper beef burgers. Your final model can also be grilled, filling your house with the pleasing aroma of tramps' socks.

A. Morris,
London

AMAZON.CO.UK. If someone purchases an exercise bike from your website, don't bother sending them endless e-mails recommending further exercise bikes. They tend not to be things you buy on a regular basis.

Christina Martin,
e-mail

HOMEOWNERS. When selling your house, replace your furniture with children's tables and chairs, and use a dwarf estate agent. Instantly, your house will seem more roomy than it actually is.

Derek Nerrington,
e-mail

MUMS. Keep everyone guessing about whether or not you have just sworn at your children by not saying "...And that's swearing!" after you have just sworn at them.

Guy,
Nottingham

WHEN visiting a service station for a cup of tea and a slice of cake, make sure you arrange your bank loan or second mortgage before you get to the tills, thus saving time and embarrassment.

Russell Dundee,
e-mail

BRIDES-TO-BE. Convince your beau that he is in for a lifetime of A1 banging by sucking his cock whilst wearing suspenders and a basque. You can always slip into something more comfortable such as thick tights, vests and pyjamas after the honeymoon.

Major McKidderminster,
Kidderminster

DEAF people. Wearing oven gloves outdoors is an ideal way to stop strangers from eavesdropping on your conversation.

Ian Knott,
Working

IF YOU find yourself nervous at the prospect of addressing a group of senior lap-dancers, try to imagine them all fully-clothed.

Graham Elvis Winning,
e-mail

COMPETITION fans. Ensure success in postal competitions by moistening the envelopes with your helmet oil. This will, upon opening, cause the release of male pheromones which will subconsciously drive the gorgeous admin assistant to pick your entry 'entirely at random'.

Michael Ringbodger,
e-mail

CONVINCE your neighbours that evolution is working backwards by not shaving for a week, walking to your car gradually more stooped each morning and wearing a monkey costume on the Friday.

Baruch Soloman,
e-mail

FOOL workmates into thinking that your father hails from Italy by walking around saying things like "Mama mia!…as my dad would say."

Jimmy Rey,
e-mail

DETER organ thieves from stealing your innards by swallowing several mousetraps minutes before your death.

Dean Rigg,
e-mail

BIG Brother winners. After having every fart, shit and piss broadcast to the nation, keep what little dignity you have left by not releasing a piss-poor single at Christmas.

Treeve Menear,
Penzance

MAKERS of Anchor Spreadable Butter. Save time and printing ink by simply calling it 'Anchor Butter.'

Richard Daw,
Hereford

A WARM stream of piss makes an excellent lightsaber for slaying snowmen who have fallen to the dark side.

Adrian Garford,
e-mail

MECHANICS. A pencil makes an absolutely perfect, if somewhat fragile, replacement for a 8mm allen key.

Thomas Thomas,
e-mail

LECTURERS. Clear nail varnish makes ideal tippex for correcting mistakes on overhead transparencies.

P A Hallows,
Manchester

HOSPITAL patients. Arrive for your appointment two hours after the assigned arrival time. That way, you will only have to wait an hour for your doctor to see you.

Dr Grim,
e-mail

CAN'T afford to see your favourite band in concert? Simply go and see a tribute band whilst wearing a beekeeper's hat. Peering through the thick mesh it will be impossible to tell you are not watching the real thing.

Emma & Ali,
London

DAILY Mail editors. Underline important words in your headlines just to make sure that your readers are clear about what it is you want them to think.

H. Barrow,
Tooting

MAKE your own carrots by painting parsnips orange.

Der Schturmer,
e-mail

BOOKSHOP owners. Annoy Christians by putting the Bible in the 'Fiction' section of your shop where, joking aside, it actually belongs.

T. Rumpole, Bailey

ANGLERS. Have both of your arms surgically extended by 4ft to add extreme exaggeration when describing the size of your catch.

Prof. Phil McCaverty, e-mail

IF YOU want your mother-in-law never to come back to your house, buy her a razor for Christmas.

Dave Oxendale, York

PROSTITUTES. If selling your body for sex makes you feel cheap, then simply raise your prices.

Tony Fisher, Ipswich

ASTRONAUTS. If contemplating another moon landing, increase your chance of success by travelling there when the moon is full.

Chris Higson, e-mail

ACTORS. Increase your chances of appearing in a Richard Curtis film by being Hugh Grant or Colin Firth.

John Cohen, e-mail

GRATED cheddar cheese from the supermarket can be squashed tightly together with the fingers to produce a block of cheese, ready for slicing or grating.

Reginald, e-mail

A MIXTURE of sour cream and mashed-up blackberries makes excellent imitation bird shit to apply to your neighbour's car after he's washed it.

Woody,
Walsall

BAKERS. Avoid confusion and imprisonment when carrying desserts through airport customs by referring to Almond and Mocha bombs as Almond and Mocha "upside-down cakes".

M. Kipling,
Guantanamo Bay

OLD people. Avoid flu-jab embarrassment by not pulling your trousers down whilst the nurse is away getting your jab. It is administered via the arm these days.

Duncan,
e-mail

JOHN Wayne. Never show any pain when receiving the beating of a lifetime, but wince when having your wounds tended by a woman.

Oggerina,
e-mail

PEOPLE ON Eastenders. Don't talk to stall owners or they will make you mind their stall while they go off and settle a score of some sort.

Martin Christian,
e-mail

IF YOU see curly-headed funnyman Alan Davies in the street, don't take his photograph as he recently told reporters that it really annoys him.

Rhiannon Collier,
Newcastle

A SOMBRERO in a bin liner makes a trendy 'hands-free' umbrella.

Bernard Eccles,
e-mail

DRIVERS. If you catch a service station assistant drinking from a bottle of water, simply wink at her, laughingly asking if it's vodka. Even the most difficult day will be lightened by your chirpy humour.

Rosemary,
Billericay

COMMUTERS. When reading a hardback book on the train to work, turn the dust jacket upside down to convince fellow passengers that you have inverted vision.

John Callaghan,
Reading

ALDI. Having tried your 'deep-filled' mince pies, I think the expression you're looking for is 'air-filled'.

William,
E-mail

GENTLEMEN. Save money on expensive dating agencies. Simply stand across the road from your local lonely hearts club and when you see someone you like come out, follow them home at a discreet distance. After they have entered their home, leave a dignified amount of time before knocking on their door and asking them out for a drink.

Stewart Cowley,
London

NATURALISTS. Make your own otter by doing bonsai on a seal.

Julian Barlow,
Coggeshall

TIGHT-ARSED blokes. During Spring and Summer, only date girls called Natalie, Carol, Holly or Eve. Chances are their birthday is around Christmas and you won't have to shell out for a present until then, by which time they will probably have packed you in.

David Bushell,
e-mail

SPECTACLE wearers. Whilst having your morning shit, take a piece of toilet paper, clean your glasses, and then wipe your arse. Hey presto, two uses for the one sheet of paper. NB. It must be done in that order.

Ian Thewlis,
Leeds

FORMER 10cc member Lol Creme. When text-messaging bad news, it is probably best not to add your name at the end as this may cause offence.

Stuart Penney,
e-mail

COMMUTERS. Why pay 20p for the use of the toilet at Waterloo when the code to use the bogs in the station's Reef Bar is 1009?

Daniel Morrison,
e-mail

AIR FRANCE. Avoid paying compensation to passengers whose bags you have lost by simply not replying to any of their letters or e-mails. Chances are it won't be worth their while pursuing you through the courts.

T Bradbury,
Winchester

RELUCTANT ARTISTS. If you want an excuse to put off starting a pencil drawing, simply have a letter, Top Tip or Profanisaurus entry published in Viz. The idle bastards will never bother sending your pencil, so you can avoid commencing your drawing indefinitely.

Nick Pettigrew,
London

SMOKERS. Take a tip from tumble dryer users. Enjoy a crafty fag at your desk by attaching a flexible vent hose to your face and running it out of the office window.

Aston Martini,
London

DEAD hedgehogs make ideal teddy bears for young bed-of-nails enthusiasts.

Mrs J. Tart,
Eccles

NEWLYWEDS. Act in a surreptitious manner from the start of your marriage so as not to attract suspicion when you do have an affair.

Joel Young,
Middlesbrough

IN YOUR early twenties, yet remarkably unfit? Simply dye your hair grey so everything you do appears young and spritely.

Russell Antcliff,
Loch Neigh

SHOPPERS. When buying oranges, get more for your money by peeling them before taking them to the counter to be weighed.

Jason Orange,
Manchester

TREASURERS from social clubs. Rather than take the flack for bad book-keeping, accuse the bar-steward of theft.

Grant Warner,
New Malden

RE-COUP some of the fortune you've spent on overpriced Viz comics over the years by auctioning your bog-smelling old ones online and lying about both their condition and rarity.

Chris,
e-mail

TOUPEE wearers. A duck placed on your head makes a warm and waterproof alternative to your usual syrup on those rainy days. For gentlemen with larger heads, try a small goose.

T. Dude,
e-mail

REMOVE lice cheaply and easily by putting onion juice on your head. Wait a few moments until the lice rub their eyes and simply fall off your head.

S. Hughes, e-mail

CRAIG David. Avoid having dog shit smeared all over the bonnet of your Porsche 911 in the Royal Well car park by not saying "My minders will fucking muller you if you bump into me again" to drinkers in Time Nightclub, Cheltenham.

Brown Hands, Cheltenham

CONTACT lens wearers. Keep your eyes snug and warm this winter by adding a few drops of chilli sauce to your cleaning solution.

Garry Kidwell, Stoke

KEEP wives and girlfriends on their toes by telling them they are the fattest girl you have ever been out with.

Hapag Lloyd, Runcorn

HUSBANDS. Get your wife to swallow your spunk by simply wanking into the milk before making her a cup of tea.

Michael Smyth, e-mail

PEOPLE in Cheltenham. When smearing dogshit on Craig David's Porsche 911 in the Royal Well car park, make sure you get plenty under the door handles and not just on the bonnet.

I. Purdy, e-mail

DOCTORS. Tired of licking stamps? Simply attach your stamps to the underside of your tongue stick before the patient says "Aah." Hey presto! Free saliva.

Moe, e-mail

HOUSEWIVES. The handy, resealable bags that Cathedral cheese comes in can be re-used to keep some nice cheese in.

Scotty, e-mail

SAVE money on water rates by only ever eating bananas, the food you can eat without washing your hands after a piss or a dump.

Arnold Verrall, Essex

DON'T throw away old socks. They can be used to protect cucumbers, marrows and aubergines from early frosts.

A. Titmarsh, Harrogate

SHOPPERS. When buying grapes, take one grape to the till. When it is weighed it won't register on the low-tech unsensitive scales so you will get it for free. Repeat this procedure a hundred times or so, and hey, presto! You have yourself a free bunch of grapes.

A. Bomb & Wan Kin Gai, Hiroshima

SKATEBOARDERS. When buying trousers, choose a pair which stop around about your ankles as opposed to some point about 10 inches further on.

Ben Keen, Whitley Bay

REDUCE the risk of night-time fire by soaking all your furniture with a hosepipe before going to bed.

Gegsey, e-mail

UGLY birds. Become better looking by simply moving North.

Andy Inman, Inverness

 # PAUL 'HUNK' HOGAN'S HAIRY TOP LIPS

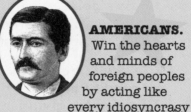 **AMERICANS.** Win the hearts and minds of foreign peoples by acting like every idiosyncrasy of their culture is hilarious, like it's a show put on for your benefit.

Ngitibulu Ng, e-mail

 WIFE beaters. When hitting your wife, get hold of a crocodile, a string of sausages and a policeman to recreate some of that seaside magic for the kids.

Michael Edwards, Stockton-on-Tees

 **BIRD** lovers. Save money on wild bird food this winter by fitting a bird feeder to the inside of your window. You only need to fill it once, but you will enjoy watching the birds at your window every day!

Lee Nelson, Stockton-on-Tees

 **PARENTS.** Half a cocktail stick with a blob of nail varnish on the end makes an ideal "safety match" that your children can play with without the risk of setting fire to anything.

Spud, Luton

 SUCCESSFUL businessmen. Fool neighbours into thinking you are unemployed by getting up everyday at 4 in the afternoon, putting on a tracksuit smeared with chocolate stains and sitting in the park drinking Kestrel Super.

Nick Smith, Leeds

 **MEN.** Can't get a blow job? Simply strip bollock-naked, plonk yourself arse-first into an empty dustbin, and you should be able to do it yourself. Use a pile of tyres instead of a dustbin if you require deep throat.

Allen Bethell, e-mail

 **PUTTING** your wife's perfume in the freezer for 2 hours, then drinking the separated alcohol makes explaining why you would do such a thing a whole lot easier.

Olly Sherman, e-mail

BODYBUILDERS. Strands of cooked spaghetti draped all over your body give your muscles that 'ripped' look that will be the envy of everyone at the gym.

Spud, Luton

 **INTERNET** porn fans. Avoid tedious interruptions to wipe the screen by first covering it with several layers of cling film which can be torn off like F1 drivers do with their visors.

Neil Priestley, e-mail

Fop Tips

FELLAS. Avoid having to do a single day's work in your life by simply wooing and marrying a queen.
*P. Mountbatten,
London*

TRAINSPOTTERS. Type the name of the train you wish to spot into an internet search engine to bring up a picture of it. You can use the time you save to get on with your life.
*Senor Beeftrotter,
e-mail*

CITY-LINK Couriers. maintain good relations with your account holders by assuring them that their next urgent package sent from Leeds to York won't end up in France.
*Lee Marks,
e-mail*

PHILANTHROPISTS. Be careful when giving street alcoholics money for 'a cup of tea', as some of the less scrupulous ones may be tempted to spend it on strong liquor.
*Mark Jordan,
e-mail*

WINDOW CLEANERS. When agreeing a price with Dr Who to clean the windows of the Tardis, don't be conned into agreeing to do the insides for the same price.
*Grant B Warner,
New Malden*

MOTORISTS. Save a fortune on expensive repair bills by simply turning your radio full blast whenever your engine makes a funny noise.
*S Poole,
Bushey*

TV BOSSES. Improve the quality of live TV news by giving 'roving reporters' the sack on air if they say 'erm...' more than three times in a single report.
*Mark Glover,
Coventry*

READERS. Don't waste money buying a copy of Bridget Jones' Diary. Simply dig out your twenty-year-old copy of The Diary of Adrian Mole and cross out all the references to 'spots, replacing them with 'fat arse'.
*Chris Cowen,
e-mail*

TRANSSEXUALS. Make yourself feel more like a woman by driving a car badly whilst talking bollocks.
*Grant B. Warner,
New Malden*

HELP to replenish the world's oxygen supply by taking a deep breath of city smog and breathing out near a tree.
*Dazza,
e-mail*

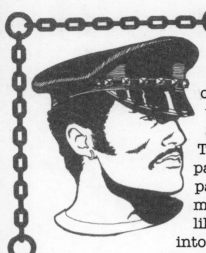

BIKERS. Remember to give two or three blips of your throttle, when stopping at the pub. This will remind patrons on the patio that you master a beast, likely to burst into life at any moment, of its own volition.

Chrispy,
e-mail

OLD ladies. A dab of silver model aircraft paint transforms repulsive facial warts into fashionable piercings.

Robert Stuart,
London

WIVES. If your husband is pestering you for a hand job and you can't be bothered, simply sit on your hand for ten minutes until it goes dead, and it will feel like someone else is doing it.

Rob Leese Jones,
e-mail

DON'T waste money buying Lo-salt. Normal salt is the same height and twice as tasty.

J. Reichelt,
e-mail

PARSNIP lovers. Save money by buying cheaper carrots and boiling them in water containing a little bleach.

James Turnip,
e-mail

JAMES Cameron. Save millions on expensive CGI for the next Avatar film by simply painting the presenters of East Midlands Today blue.

Simon Snore,
e-mail

RECREATE the danger of a parachute jump in safety by visiting Google Earth and clicking the scroll bar until you reach the ground. Add realism to the exercise by putting a fan on blowing full in your face.

Christian Frank,
Billingham

OWNERS of sandwich shops in Diamond Street, Aberdeen who run out of bread at 12.15 every day. Instead of advising hungry customers to arrive earlier, why not simply order more bread?

Brian,
e-mail

HOUSEWIVES. Feel like a Hollywood celebrity by fitting red carpets in every room in your house. A trip to the toilet will feel like attending a film premiere.

T. Jenkins,
Grange Hill

JURY foremen. Add reality-TV-style suspense to your verdict by saying "We the jury find the defendant..." and then leaving a two-minute pause before delivering the outcome whilst another jury member plays a low roll on a kettle drum.

Edna Spinosa,
Newant

HARVEY Nichols customers. When entering the shop, always have a large wad of money in your hand so that the doorman and other staff will see that you can afford their stuff and won't look at you as if you're something that's just dropped off a tramp's arse.

Ted Bartlett,
e-mail

A ROAST sparrow makes an ideal Christmas dinner turkey for a family of mice who wear clothes. I don't know what they could use for crackers, though.

Victor Giraffe,
e-mail

TRANSVESTITES. Make a more convincing woman by dressing in a polar fleece, saggy track suit bottoms and trainers and dragging three kids around a supermarket.

Heather,
e-mail

A FEW conkers threaded on an old bootlace makes an inexpensive 'love bead' sex toy to surprise your wife with on her next birthday.

Philip O'Carroll,
e-mail

EPILEPTICS. Next time you have a seizure, check yourself in the toilet mirror afterwards to make sure your best friends haven't drawn glasses on your face with a marker pen to the amusement of the rest of the nightclub.

J. Roo,
e-mail

WASPS make ideal doormen for beehives.

Bill Broonzy,
e-mail

SLOVENLY householders. Always keep a few 'Get Well Soon' cards on the mantlepiece. When unexpected visitors arrive you can tell them that you have not been well and that's why the house is untidy.

Maz,
e-mail

SHOPPERS. If what you wish to purchase is not in stock, inform the assistant that you've come all the way from Stanely on the No.2 bus. They will take pity on you and have your item materialise out of thin fucking air.

Johnny,
e-mail

THAT LITTLE bald-headed bloke off the Benny Hill Show. Next time Benny Hill slaps you rapidly on the head, hit the fat fucker back. Bullies don't pick on people who stand up to them

Fat Al White,
Wrenthorpe

SAINSBURYS. Make a mockery of your 'We have removed carrier bags from our tills' scheme by instructing your cashiers to offer every customer some of the bags hidden under their seats.

Andrew Stevens,
Manchester

OLD people. Feeling lonely, isolated and ignored? Simply advertise a car in the Autotrader for £2000 below the list price and Hey Presto! Your phone won't stop ringing for a month.

Peter Britton,
e-mail

MC Hammer's STOP... Tips Time!

NERVOUS people. Never chew the inside of your cheeks whilst on high-strength prescription painkillers.

Matt Hindley,
e-mail

FEEL a bit like God for the day by making some little people out of plasticine, and then judging them harshly.

Hector Plywood,
Devizes

A SERIES of quiet burps in your sleeping wife's ear will ensure she has pleasant dreams about burps. Similar results can be achieved with farts.

Kelly,
Ulsan

GIVE your office that fabric shop feel by pushing all the desks together and fixing rulers along one edge with blu-tac.

Superjohn,
e-mail

TWO ladybirds glued together make an ideal bowling ball for a doll's house bowling alley.

T Wardrobe,
e-mail

HUGE multi-national companies. Instead of employing highly paid IT departments simply buy a consignment of parrots and teach them to say 'turn it off and then on again'.

Tim Ogden,
e-mail

LADIES, save money on sexy lace underwear by stapling paper doilies to your usual underwear.

Pete Turner,
e-mail

FAT partygoers. Your overloaded plate is more likely to go undetected if you don't sing, whistle or hum with delight at the buffet.

Macker,
e-mail

A GLASS mixing bowl turned upside down over a saucer of water in the garden makes an ideal Centre Parcs for ants.

Mike,
e-mail

VINYL enthusiasts. Re-create that old fashioned stuck needle sound when listening to an mp3 on your computer by occasionally pressing CTRL+ALT+DEL mid song.

Mike Harbidge,
e-mail

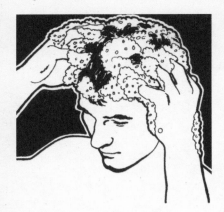

BT. When customers e-mail you to complain that you haven't activated the call-answering system that they ordered, e-mail them back saying that you phoned them to discuss the problem but couldn't leave a message.

*David Orton,
e-mail*

ALCOHOLICS. Pretend your life is one big episode of Cheers by inviting the postman and a psychiatrist around for drinks every afternoon.

*Chris Hanson,
e-mail*

WHEN having a pizza delivered, call the shop back after it has arrived and tell them that it's the wrong one. Minutes later, another pizza will be delivered. They will not ask for the old pizza back because it is their policy as they don't know what you have done to it. Hey presto! Two pizzas for the price of one.

*Paul Gillespie,
e-mail*

MASTURBATORS. Create the effect that you've been sleeping on your arm by getting someone else to pull you off.

*John Dobson,
e-mail*

WIG wearers. Don't waste money on new wigs. Simply turn your old ones round for that 'boy band' look.

*Danny the Dog,
e-mail*

MOD SCIENTISTS. Make cheap body armour out of sweetcorn. If it's strong enough to survive the commute through my guts, I reckon it could probably stop a bullet.

*Ed O'Meara,
e-mail*

TWINS. Always make your twin try on a new outfit before you buy it so you can see exactly how you will look in it. (This does not work if your twin is of the opposite sex. Unless you are a drag queen. Or the opposite of a drag queen).

*Matt Jones
Cambridge*

MCDONALD'S. Double the amount of money your customers donate to children's charities by reducing the cost of your breakfast from £1.99 to £1.98.

*Dave Saunders,
Cricklewood*

SAVE money on window cleaning by covering your windows in clingfilm and removing it when dirty.

*Lisa Stout,
e-mail*

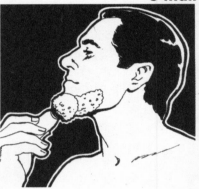

GIRLS. Make people think you are a nurse by growing a massive arse.

*A. Miller,
Leeds*

CREATE that 'just been to the swimming pool' feeling by spraying yourself with bleach, rubbing chilli sauce in your eyes and stuffing your ears with Blu-Tac.

*Rob Cottam,
e-mail*

NEED a day off work? Convince your boss you have a cold over the phone by slipping your tongue into a boiling hot Pop Tart before you call.

*Andy Mapps,
e-mail*

SUDOKU lovers. Solve your puzzles in seconds by logging on to http://sudoku.sourceforge.net/, typing the clues into the grid and clicking the 'solve' button. This will save hours, leaving you plenty of time to do something worthwhile.

T Wensleydale,
Cheshire

DAILY Express editors. Test your readers' memories by constantly filling your paper with inflammatory articles about asylum seekers and immigrants and then feigning disgust when the BNP gets elected.

Mark,
e-mail

DRIVING towards a red light sufficiently fast will cause the 'blue shift' effect, making it appear green, allowing you to go straight over.

Paul Bullough,
e-mail

A DOG turd bent into a U shape makes a great magnet for flies.

S Nutkin,
Stoke

CAR owners. Dissuade humorous neighbours from saying "you can do mine next!" when you're cleaning your car by keeping a hammer in your pocket and starting to batter your windscreen when you see them approaching.

Geoff Owens,
e-mail

HAIRDRESSERS. Break even during the recession by not cutting your customers' hair so short. They'll be back for another chop in no time and you can charge them again.

Richard,
Ross-on-Wye

FELLAS. Don't waste money on expensive pornographic magazines. Simply ask female friends to pose naked whilst you masturbate.

Neil Keenan,
e-mail

AQUARIUM owners. Slow your fish down to a more therapeutic pace by filling your tank with clear hair gel.

Craig Eddie,
e-mail

ELDERLY ladies. Ensure maximum delay for motorists by in the high street by conducting conversations beside zebra crossings.

Tim Dorrington,
e-mail

DAILY Mail editors. Confuse your readers by claiming that asylum seekers are the natural predators of paedophiles.

Tommy Dungmonger,
e-mail

MICHAEL PARKINSON. Take your thorny-issue-avoiding interview style to its ultimate conclusion by inviting Osama Bin Laden onto your show and asking him for funny anecdotes about life on the road.

G. Dyke,
On his Bike

DIZZEE Rascal. It is possible that you are suffering from an inner ear disorder. A GP-initiated consultation with an otolaryngologist should have you back on your feet in no time.

Gary Parslow,
e-mail

TRAMPS. make passers-by think you are eloquent by sipping your Buckfast with your pinky finger pointing out.

**Harold Ramp,
St Pancras Station**

WIDOWER motorists. Place your SatNav on a long plank of wood protruding from the back of your car. The spoken directional instructions will then be delivered at the exact moment you have missed your intended turning, thus bringing back fond memories of your late wife's attempts at map reading.

**Larry Olden,
e-mail**

MIDGETS. Appear taller by snacking on fun-size Mars bars and speaking very quietly, thus giving the impression that you are merely a long way away.

**J Barton,
e-mail**

ALARM clock owners. Save money on batteries by drinking 12 pints of ale the night before, then setting your arse to fart loudly in a sleep/snooze pattern between 7.00 and 8.00 o'clock the following morning.

**Marc Rats,
e-mail**

PARENTS. Confuse your children by taking them to Great Yarmouth's outdated House of Wax, where they will invariably ask 'Who's Barry Sheene?'

**Mandy Pearson,
e-mail**

SMOKERS. When non-smokers visit your house, ask them to stand outside in the cold whilst you have a fag.

**Desi Friel,
e-mail**

ITV news readers. Introduce news scares about legal drugs by using the words 'suspected', 'possible' and 'we understand' repeatedly. This will save you having to actually research any true facts.

**Chris Hardy,
e-mail**

TORCH owners. When looking for your torch in the dark, avoid wasting batteries in a second torch by just waiting until it's light to look for it.

**Grant B Warner,
New Zealand**

IF YOU are over 10 metres in front of someone, don't hold the door open for them. You're not doing them a favour, you're just making them run.

**Christina Martin,
e-mail**

AVOID being punched in the nose the next time you plan to insult somebody by simply saying 'No disrespect, but...,' at the start of your sentence. It never fails to bamboozle the victim.

**Fluff Freeman,
e-mail**

MEN. Pretend you have a sex drive until your girlfriend moves in with you. Then wear 15-year-old band T-shirts in bed whilst reading Tintin books.

**Rabbit's Best Friend,
e-mail**

IF YOU'VE had a particularly hot curry and cold toilet paper isn't working, try applying some lipsalve to the affected ring piece, it works a treat. Just don't try to be a clever dick and put it back in my handbag after you've done so.

**Leigh-Ann Dee,
e-mail**

TOPPER TIPS

WOMEN. Discourage men from looking at your breasts by wearing a skirt short enough to see your knickers.

*Dick Swindles,
e-mail*

TAXPAYERS. Beat the taxman by only ever doing a job for three months, then resigning and signing on for the next three months. That way, you get back the tax you paid while you were working.

*H. R.,
e-mail*

GEOGRAPHY teachers. Attach pitta bread to the elbows of your tweed jacket for a tasty alternative to leather patches.

*Chris Miller,
e-mail*

HOUSEWIVES. When washing clothes, pop a couple of tea-bags in the washer instead of soap powder, milk where the fabric conditioner should go and put it on a boil wash. Hey presto, when the clothes are washed you can enjoy a nice cup of tea.

*Adam Smith,
Bradford*

GEORDIES. Protect yourself from bird flu by dressing the Angel of the North up like a giant scarecrow.

*Craig Roberts,
e-mail*

MUMS. Put your feet up when your husband comes home from work and let him deal with the kids. After all, you've had a busy day at 'Tea & Tots' talking about his piles.

Dan,
e-mail

ENGLISH Defence League members. When holding signs reading 'Ban The Burka', you might want to reconsider wearing a balaclava so as not to appear overly hypocritical.

Johnny Adair,
e-mail

TV MANUFACTURERS. Now that TVs have a helpful display enabling us to 'see' how loud the volume is, why not add a constant bleeping sound which gets higher of lower in pitch as we adjust the brightness?

Johnny Two Spoons,
e-mail

FAT, balding blokes in your 50s. Don't buy Porsche 911s as you may look a bit of a twat when struggling to climb out of them at Tesco petrol stations.

Nick Bullen,
e-mail

PICKLED onions make ideal breast implants for cats.

Mark French,
e-mail

MAKE it appear that you have twice as many things as you actually have by standing them all in front of a mirror.

N Bohr,
London

MAKE passers-by think your dog is a robot by feeding it a roll of tin foil before taking it for a dump in the local park.

David Milner,
Durham

MAKE it appear that you have an infinite number of things by placing them directly in-between two mirrors parallel to each other.

N Bohr,
London

LONDON Zoo. Attract more visitors by putting some animals in the cages.

Mickey Sparkle,
e-mail

BLEND parmesan cheese, basil, olive oil, and hay. Hey presto! Hay pesto.

Edd Almond,
e-mail

THE VATICAN. Prevent the Pope's assassination by replacing him with a giant glove puppet. You can never see his feet anyway and the speeches would probably make more sense too.

P Matic,
e-mail

SHIFT workers. Can't get to sleep during the day because it's too light? Simply take a wind-up torch to bed, turn it on and wind the handle the wrong way.

Patrick Brogan,
e-mail

AFTER a shite, wipe with a baby wipe instead of toilet roll. That way, you wash your arse and your hands at the same time, thus saving an unnecessary trip to the sink.

Tiger,
e-mail

SPRAY fish and chips with Mr Muscle window cleaner. It contains vinegar and will cut through grease, leaving your meal more healthy.

Bartram Laidlaw,
Crewe

GIRLS. Recreate your favourite scenes from Sex & The City by strapping your tits to your knees and going to a café to talk utter bollocks with three of your mates.

Kirk Jones, e-mail

CONVINCE people that you are a secret service agent by attaching a piece of curly telephone cable to your ear and occasionally raising your hand to it while frowning.

Martyn Goodram, Bolton

ALL YOUR bowls in the dishwasher? An old trilby hat turned upside down makes an ideal salad bowl for dry salad. For soup, try the appropriately-named 'bowler' hat, but line it first with a real bowl to stop the soup seeping out.

Renton Boyce, Torquay

OUT OF WORK actors. Simply pretend that you have a job and, hey presto! You're working.

Ben Margerison e-mail

KRAFT cheese slices make ideal patches for heavy cheese eaters who are trying to cut down.

Fish, Axminster

INCREASE the size of your rooms by decorating them with thinner wallpaper.

Tony Dewey, e-mail

HAIR straighteners make an ideal grill for one fish finger.

Alex Dyer, e-mail

VIBRATiNG cock rings make excellent shock collars for naughty ferrets and other small rodents.

Naomi Willett, e-mail

TOP TIPS the only page you read in Viz? Save money by simply taking a photograph of that particular page whilst reading it in Sainsburys.

Joe Park, e-mail

A DOUBLE oven mitt draped over your dog's back makes ideal 'saddle bags' enabling your pet to carry items like cans of beer, telly remote controls, etc.

Steve White, e-mail

GLASSES wearers. Get the same effect as upgrading to an expensive HD television by simply giving your lenses a wipe.

Rick M, e-mail

FELLAS. Stand outside an Ann Summers shop dressed in a security guard's uniform with a smoke detector in your pocket. When a fit bird walks out, simply press the smoke alarm test button and voila! A free grope!

D Clegg, Cirencester

RESTAURATEURS.
Draw attention away from your cuisine being bland, tasteless and overpriced by serving it on an oversized, wavy oblong plate.

Stuart Achilles,
e-mail

VACUUM cleaner nozzles make great intergalactic 'wormholes' for spiders and woodlice.

Woof the wolf,
e-mail

SAVE money on alarm clocks by living next door to twats.

Christina Martin,
e-mail

CLOSET gays trapped in straight marriage. Sellotape a pair of glasses just above your wife's pubes. Vaginal sex will then look like you are getting a blower off a man with a beard.

Pete Howies,
e-mail

REPLACEMENT clothes line too long? Measure it to find the extra length, then simply knock your house down and rebuild it the requisite distance from your linen post.

Paul Arger,
e-mail

PRETEND you are at a rally for enthusiasts of normal, everyday cars by driving to a supermarket car park and sitting beside your vehicle in a folding chair, talking about it to everyone who passes.

R Belfitt,
Leeds

HUSBANDS. Prevent accusations of being impolite or discourteous in the bedroom by simply saying 'Excuse me love, would you mind passing me the fanny?' to your wife. It works every time.

Steve Bates,
e-mail

RATIONAL thinkers. Test your self-control by listening to Thought for the Day on Radio 4, while trying to refrain from laughing out loud or shouting 'bullshit' at the radio.

Mike Tatham,
e-mail

CHEESE eaters. Instead of eating a large piece of mild cheese, save time and money by eating a much smaller piece of extra mature cheese.

Shenkin Arsecandle,
e-mail

VACUUM cleaner manufacturers. Install headphone ports into your products, then only the user will have to put up with the noise.

Malcolm Alcock,
e-mail

ACTION heroes. Save money on guns by not throwing them on the floor the moment they run out of ammunition.

Adam Gatward,
e-mail

HOLLYWOOD directors. If the action jumps to Paris, have an onscreen caption saying 'Paris, France' over an establishing shot of the Eiffel Tower just in case the audience think you mean some other fucking Paris.

Carlos
e-mail

TOP FLIPS

BY GRABBING hold of a charity letter and twisting it sideways, it is possible to remove the free pen without opening it and subjecting yourself to all that guilt.

Phil Hunt,
Stroud

VERY OLD people in nursing homes. Go to bed each night in a suit and lie on your back with your arms crossed neatly over your chest. This could save a fair amount of money on undertakers' fees.

Fred Funk,
e-mail

LIVEN up boring golf tournaments by occasionally blowing a vuvuzela just as the golfer is driving off the tee.

Jeremy of Estonia,
e-mail

MAKE YOUR OWN SNOW BY WAFTING STEAM FROM THE KETTLE INTO THE FREEZER AND QUICKLY SLAMMING THE DOOR.

ROB STOTT,
E-Mail

STUDENTS. DEMONSTRATE YOUR DRINKING PROWESS BY PILING UP BOTTLES AND CANS ON YOUR WINDOW LEDGE. THIS IS SURE TO IMPRESS YOUR HARSHEST CRITICS AND HAVE THE BEST-LOOKING BIRDS BEATING A PATH TO YOUR DOOR.

MIKE TATHAM,
E-MAIL

GUINNESS World Record Fans. Don't bother shoving Smarties under your foreskin as apparently they will not accept this as a world record.

Gareth D,
e-mail

MOTORISTS. Buy four wheel clamps from Argos for £15 each, park anywhere you like and attach them to your car. Wardens will be unable to attach any more clamps and it is still cheaper than the release fee.

Pete A,
e-mail

RA-SPBERRIES MAKE EXCELLENT AFROS FOR MICE. THEY ARE ALSO VERY TASTY.

DUCKIN FULLARD,
GARFORTH

HOUSEWIVES. Make the normally mundane task of switching the central heating on a little more exciting by singing "The heating's on" to the tune of 80s hit The Heat is On by Glen Frey as you are doing it.

Jorgen Jarlesberg,
Goole

FOOL WOMEN into thinking you HAVE A WELL PAID job in the animal testing industry by throwing paint stripper over your car.

Simon TENA-LADY,
E-MAIL

BIRD watchers. Get a closer look at birds by shooting them, then picking them up for inspection.

George Belcher,
e-mail

ROUND dodgers. Saying 'Do you want a pint or are you alright?' Makes it so uncomfortable for the recipient that they will invariably decline your 'kind' offer.

Fluff Freeman,
e-mail

COUNTDOWN contestants. Always choose consonants for your first three letters so that sad, unemployed male viewers can get a good view of Rachael's bottom as she twists to lift them.

Hugh Beaforte, e-mail

DROPPED some peas and suffering from pins and needles in your hands? Simply pick the peas up one at a time by sucking at them through a drinking straw.

Pertree Shackleton, Launceston

DON'T throw away the lids off yoghurt pots. Simply stick them onto the top of dowdy shoes to jazz them up.

Toby Yarwood, Thirsk

DON'T throw out that old record player. It makes an ideal revolving serving platter for cakes, where diners can pick a cake as it spins by. Set it to 33rpm for rock cakes and scones, 45rpm for Eccles cakes and Battenburg and 78 rpm for Danish pastries.

Betty Prolapse, Pontyprydd

TEENAGERS. Shave minutes off your daily routine by forcing your face into a colander to burst your acne.

Lund Humphries, e-mail

FOOL your girlfriend into thinking that you don't fancy her identical twin sister by telling her that you think she is ugly.

John W, e-mail

SCULPTORS. When designing a new statue for your city centre, why not add a stone traffic cone to its head to discourage pissed students from risking death at 3.00 am.

Garry Smith, East Kilbride

KEEP wooden chip shop forks, plastic holly decorations and broken birthday candles somewhere handy. We keep ours at the back of the tea towel drawer.

Ed Surname, e-mail

EAST Sussex Council. Save money on cleaning up graffiti by changing the name of the River Uck to the River Fuck and be done with.

Christina Martin, e-mail

POST OFFICE counter staff. If the queue in your post office is too small, make sure you try to sell insurance, mobile phone top ups and any other useless shite you can think of to anyone who just wants to buy a stamp. In no time at all you'll have the poor buggers queueing out of the door and down the street again.

John Smith, e-mail

NIGELLA Lawson fans. In a few years time, the sexy cook will start to sag and probably end up looking like her dad Nigel in a dress. I only mention it because this information will help you last a bit longer the next time you wank at the telly.

James Leicester, e-mail

JEREMY Kyle. Avoid causing offence when speaking to the vermin on your show by saying 'I'm not judging you' before slagging them off. This will also enable the twats in the audience to nod in a superior manner.

Phil,
e-mail

TRAINSPOTTERS. Mingle with normal people on the station platform. You can record the train numbers just as easily as you could standing on the end of the platform, which only makes you a target for scorn and ridicule.

Fat Al White,
Wrenthorpe

CONDEMNED prisoners. Listen to Duncan Barkes's night-time Ultimate Late Show Live phone-in on Talksport during your last night before being put to death. It will make your final hours stretch out endlessly, and cause you to actively welcome the arrival of your executioner in the morning.

John Pearson,
Leeds

ANGRY teenagers. Save time self-harming by simply shaving with a Bic razor whilst getting ready for a night out.

Tony Anstis,
e-mail

BIRDWATCHERS. String up fairy lights and tinsel to give your garden that authentic 'nightclub' look. A record player covered in seeds makes an excellent revolving dance floor, and at closing time your cat can be an effective bouncer.

Harry Cowderoy,
e-mail

HAIRDRESSERS. Instead of repeatedly asking customers parrot fashion where they are going on holiday, why not charge less for a dry trim? That way, we might be able to go further than Minehead.

Bob Trimback,
e-mail

CAN'T afford a camera for your holiday? Simply take along a friend with a photographic memory, then have them describe all those wonderful holiday memories when you get home.

Summerhead,
e-mail

OLD FOLK. Don't waste money on those over-sized uni-slippers, simply sellotape your existing slippers together. When you evening's TV viewing is finished, just cut through and remove the sellotape.

Jeremy Clarkhole,
e-mail

BAD guys. Ensure your captives are tied or handcuffed properly as a surprisingly high proportion of good guys manage to cast off their shackles.

Nicko McPhillipee,
e-mail

ACORNS wrapped in silver paper make great Easter eggs for squirrels.

Acko,
e-mail

HOUSEWIVES. Don't waste kitchen roll mopping up spilt milk. Simply place a Weetabix in the centre of the puddle to soak it up and pop it in the fridge for the following day's breakfast.

Penny Chew,
e-mail

CHEESE graters can also be used to grate carrots.

Lee Taylor,
e-mail

iPHONES make ideal iPads for midgets.

Dr Oracle,
e-mail

PS I won't bother saying that iPads make ideal iPhones for giants. I'm sure your readers could work that one out for themselves.

POLICE officers. Tackle the problem of prostitution in cities by visiting 'red light districts' and replacing all the bulbs with conventional white ones.

Elli Brodie,
e-mail

FELLAS. Pretend to be gay so you can befriend lesbian couples. Then have an affair with the cute one.

M Butch,
e-mail

CATHOLIC emos. Avoid breaking with your religious doctrine by only cutting yourself with a fish knife on Friday.

Francine Conklin,
e-mail

SADO-MASOCHISTS. Don't waste money on dominatrix prostitutes. Simply travel on a Virgin train at 5pm on a Friday. Discomfort, degradation, real danger and verbal abuse from specialists in uniform for a fraction of what you would spend in Marylebone.

Ishmael Skyes,
London

SAVE time dressing before work in the morning by getting a job in a nudist colony.

Jimbob Hotpants,
e-mail

CONVINCE your neighbours that you have had a bump in your car by sprinkling torn-up red and yellow fruit gums outside your house where you normally park.

Nick Gibson,
e-mail

A ROW of about 20 unused staples makes an ideal musical washboard for the mouse playing Corky the Policeman in a mouse version of the sitcom Sykes.

Jim Hobson,
Lytham St Annes

AMERICANS. Build your houses out of bricks and mortar instead of cheap wood to avoid having them destroyed by hurricanes every few weeks.

Craig Meredith,
e-mail

GIRLS. During the warm weather, keep your discarded pullover or jacket draped over your shoulders and not tied around your waist, as this prevents us from looking at your bottom.

P. Birkin,
London

WIVES of darts players. Put an oche in front of the toilet to minimise careless spraying.

Leftin Frefall,
e-mail

FOOL the police into thinking you have committed a crime by simply concealing one hand inside your jacket and running away each time you see them.

Michael Colling,
e-mail

ESCAPE FROM Coldtip

DOCTORS. Take a tip from shows like Search for a Star or Any Dream Will Do to make your patients' hospital visits more exciting. Say "And the results of your cancer tests are..." then leave a two-minute silence to build up the tension.

**H Moron,
Luton**

WEIGHT watchers. After reaching your ideal weight, maintain it by weighing yourself before and after a dump. The weight difference is the amount of food you can eat before having another dump.

**Nick Brook,
e-mail**

PUBLIC toilet users. When you realise the person in the next cubicle is holding fire until you leave, simply open and close the toilet door without leaving. Their first plop can then be greeted with a huge cheer.

**Sam,
e-mail**

LOTTO players. This weekend when you buy a ticket, mark the 'Wednesday' box instead of the 'Saturday' one. Then on Saturday night when none of your numbers come up, you'll have another chance to win on Wednesday.

**Richard Karslake,
Oxon**

SAVE money on expensive telephone sex lines. Simply send a text message of unadulterated filth to your own landline. Hey presto! The automatic BT text reader will then repeat back the grot of your own choice to your own front room in husky female tones.

**Ian Cramphorn,
Trousers**

BBC producers. If someone from Newcastle appears on one of your programmes, show a short montage of them walking along the Quayside with the Tyne Bridge clearly in the background. As far as I know, this has never been done before, but then again I am blind. And I don't have a television.

**Chris Scaife,
e-mail**

BANANA lovers. Buy your bananas in bunches of five on Sunday. Then arrange them in order of ripeness and write a day of the week on each banana in felt pen, Monday on the ripest, Friday on the greenest, to save time making those decisions on a hectic weekday morning.

**Mrs Facebook,
Bakewell**

HAYFEVER sufferers. Don't waste money on expensive pills and nasal sprays. Simply glue a bee to your upper lip. The insect workaholic will grab all stray pollen heading towards your nostrils and transform it into delicious honey for your morning toast.

**Stu the Gasman,
e-mail**

MALES. If stuck for something to talk about with other equally-awkward males at social gatherings, simply pipe up about a random A-road or motorway that you crossed on your journey and mention that it was 'quite busy.' This will spark off an exchange of similar road-themed anecdotes that should last until home time.

**Latchkey Wizzard,
Canterspay**

GERMAN perverts. Go to a beach in California and shout "Help! I've been stung by a jellyfish!" As the most natural remedy for this is dousing the sting in urine, you're almost guaranteed a golden shower from a gaggle of Baywatch beauties.

**Brian Eggo,
e-mail**

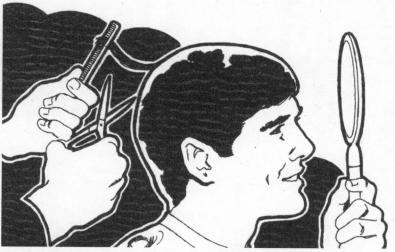

HOMEOWNERS. Don't waste money on an expensive safe. Simply keep all your valuables safe from burglars by storing them in an empty Only Fools and Horses DVD box set.

Yaxley Stilton,
Cambridge

FOOTBALL managers. Unsure how to get space in your opponents' penalty area at dead-ball situations due to tight man marking? Simply put your attackers in their own penalty area which will mean that the opposition's defence will be nowhere near their goal. Then move your defenders into attacking positions. Hey Presto! None of them will be marked. Can I be the England manager? I can speak Italian.

Alan Heath,
e-mail

GOTHS. Achieve 'the look' and help society by attending several blood donor sessions in a day. For maximum effect refuse the offer of tea and biscuits afterwards.

J McGrady,
e-mail

SAVE money on expensive bananas by mixing cold mashed potato and banana syrup.

Lawry,
e-mail

SUBBUTEO enthusiasts. Recreate the authentic World Cup 2010 atmosphere by having a paper bag full of wasps in the vicinity of your pitch.

Peter Barnes,
e-mail

DUSTMEN. Save energy by leaving my bin outside my house after you've emptied it instead of dragging it into a different postcode.

Bobby Dazzler,
e-mail

AIRBAG in your Astra gone off and can't afford to have it replaced? A Ginsters pastie fits perfectly in to the hole in the steering wheel. Not only will it give a gentle cushioning effect on impact, but it will provide you with a tasty snack while you wait for the fire brigade to cut you out of the wreckage.

Jerry Cozens,
e-mail

FOOTY fans. Fed up with watching England lose? Simply watch all their games in reverse on your Sky or Virgin box. This will ensure that all their games end in a nil-nil draw, which, let's face it, is the best they can hope for these days.

Gordon Downey,
e-mail

GENTS. Fool your penis into thinking it's having sex by shaking it vigorously whilst thinking of naked ladies.

Gary Chisholme,
e-mail

INJURED women. When in need of a double hand transplant, request those of a man. You should then be able to throw/catch balls, erect shelves, dispose of unwanted spiders, etc. You could also fondle your tits on lonely occasions and feel the warming touch of a man.

Bunty Cubbles,
e-mail

WHISTLE blowers. Guarantee anonymity by only ever using a dog whistle.

Stoner Smurf,
e-mail

SAVE water by washing your hands in the cistern of the toilet before flushing.

Barry,
e-mail

MOTORHOME owners. Instead of towing your Smart car behind your motorhome, tow your motorhome behind your Smart car as they are much more economical on fuel.

Popeymike,
e-mail

FOOL your doctor into thinking you are going on an exotic foreign holiday by making an appointment to have Malaria and Typhoid jabs.

Kevin Monster, Arbroath

RAIL passengers. Try pressing the button to open the door as the train pulls away. It won't magically open, but it will provide the driver with amusement as he watches on the CCTV.

A Traindriver, London

STOP blokes walking around with pitbulls and Staffordshires by simply changing the breed names to things like ladypuff marmalade terriers.

Tony Cockles, e-mail

HELP to teach kids how government works by simply taking all their sweets off them and telling them to fuck off.

fang, e-mail

AXL ROSE. If turning up at a venue within 2 hours of a pre-arranged time is too demanding for you, then why not consider a career with a more generous appointment window, such as a Parcel Force delivery driver or Virgin Media broadband installer?

J Davighi, e-mail

SHOPPERS. Use a 1 Euro coin in the trolley chain instead of a pound coin, saving yourself 11p at today's exchange rates. If the pound is suddenly devalued, simply do your shopping in Europe and use a pound coin.

Tony K, e-mail

SOUTHERNERS. Convince everyone you are a northerner by regularly going to the foot of your stairs.

Nigel Hurll, e-mail

SAVE time when counting to 10 by starting at the number 4. If you are in a real hurry, try starting at 5.

Ian Smith, e-mail

BONO. Take the piss by spending thousands of pounds on pink-tinted sunglasses, then ask the working class to give to charity.

Ryan P., e-mail

JEREMY Kyle show participants. 'Irregardless' is not a word. The word you are looking of is either irrespective or regardless.

Jubnut, e-mail

AVOID an entirely preventable court appearance by refraining from using the expression 'unrelenting shower of incompetent cunts' in correspondence with BT, Sky, O2, Vodaphone, Virgin Media, Virgin Trains, London Midland Trains, Northampton Borough Council, Scottish and Southern Energy, Npower and Microsoft.

J Davighi, e-mail

DON'T want to move out of your favourite armchair to make your dinner? Simply put the ingredients in a slow cooker tied to the back of a tortoise and leave a trail of lettuce leaves from the kitchen to your chair. In 6 hours time your meal will be ready and delivered to your feet.

Dave Wombat, Hull

MOTORISTS. Avoid costly road tax by simply fitting a skirt and a large fan to your car to convert it to a hovercraft. Ensure you never stop on a journey or park on the road and you won't have to pay as your 'car' never touches the road.

Terry Dactill,
e-mail

PET owners. Don't bother getting your cat neutered. Simply buy one of those rubber thimbles that bank clerks use for counting money and slip it on your moggy's lipstick. Hey presto! A catty condom. It's even ribbed for extra pleasure.

Phil Godsell,
e-mail

GENTLEMEN. An erect penis makes an ideal emergency perch for an escaped budgerigar, I would imagine.

John Rhythm,
e-mail

NEW mothers. Estimate the size your child will be when fully grown and christen them Small, Medium, Large or Extra Large accordingly. When they are older, they will automatically have their name sewn into their clothing.

Peter Cooke,
e-mail

SNOOKER players. Wear clown shoes to help get those hard-to-reach shots where you have to stretch over the table whilst keeping your feet on the floor.

Neil Mainey,
e-mail

FOOD label designers. Instead of writing 'Best before end: see top of lid, why not simply replace this message with the best before end date?

Niloc,
e-mail

GAME show and cereal enthusiasts. Recreate the madness of the end of The Crystal Maze by quickly picking all the raisins out of your muesli. But for every oat you pick up, deduct a raisin.

Jonny R,
e-mail

CRICKET fans: Save yourself some cash by fashioning a pair of cricket gloves from a pack of iced finger buns, sticking one on each of your fingers. Not only do they look like the real thing but you can eat them once you're done playing.

Electric Eric,
e-mail

GLUE some blackcurrants to your anus and go to the doctor complaining of haemorrhoids. When he gives you some ointment on prescription, it can be saved as an 'insurance policy' should you ever develop the condition for real.

Ian Smith,
e-mail

RADIO enthusiasts. Don't bother listening to commercial radio stations. Simply invite your most witless, tedious neighbour round to put records on and then talk over them.

Ed O'Meara,
e-mail

REFEREES. Keep a lie detector at the pitch side. Players know if they were offside or not, and it could sort out those tricky decisions.

Neil Vickery,
e-mail

PORN stars. Save money on anal bleaching and bum-wad by wiping your arse with disposable toilet cleaning wipes.

Ishta the Relaxed,
e-mail

AVOID the embarrassment of going for an STD check by having unprotected sex with your girlfriend, then sending her instead.

Russell Brockett,
e-mail

Tippy Egg & Soldiers

US GOVERNMENT. Repay the millions of pounds, all the lives of British soldiers and the embarrassment of everyone supporting the US invasion of Iraq by increasing the cost of paperwork needed for UK citizens to visit your country for 6 months to $600, then make them wait half-a-day at immigration and treat them like shit. Underline the irony of the situation by repeatedly banging on about how the USA has no truer friend than Great Britain.

Diccon Cooper,
e-mail

DON'T worry if your kitchen smells of farts when you're boiling eggs. Simply eat the eggs and do a fart. Hey, presto. Your kitchen will smell of eggs again.

Scaddy,
Crawley

BRITISH army. Ensure confusion amongst your troops by charging them 30p for a bottle of Becks in Hohne Garrison, Germany, then make them sit through a 30-minute lecture on the dangers of alcohol the day after a heavy session.

Rye,
e-mail

RURAL Affairs ministers. Avoid wasting eggs in public by driving to public functions in a large frying pan.

Harry the Lung,
e-mail

BOIL an egg to perfection without costly egg-timers by popping the egg into boiling water and driving away from your home at exactly 60mph. After 3 miles, phone your wife and tell her to take the egg out the pan.

James Bell,
e-mail

BOILED EGGS cut in half vertically, and with the yolk removed, make ideal miniature porcelain-style urinals for hamsters and guinea pigs.

Robert Healey,
e-mail

IN A RUSH? Cook your breakfast egg in half the time by replacing the water in the pan with commercially-available brake fluid which boils at 200°c.

Carlos,
Northern Ireland

HOUSEWIVES. Wean your husbands onto raw eggs without them realising by removing the sand from your egg timer one grain at a time.

Tim,
Brighton

AN EMPTY egg carton makes an ideal training bra for dogs.

Rob,
e-mail

FITNESS Instructors – help fat people do sit-ups by gluing Scotch eggs to the tops of their shoes.

Stu Mandry,
e-mail

RESTLESS sleepers. Fry two eggs close enough together so that they form an albumen bridge in the middle. Hey presto! You have an eye mask that you can eat the next morning.

Skodaboy,
e-mail

US TROOPS. Catch members of the Taliban by setting large mousetraps in the Tora Bora hills and baiting them with a little girl learning to read.

T Wentworth,
Rhyll

TOP TICKS

CONVINCE bar staff that your pint is off by sticking your finger up your arse before holding the glass close to their nose.

**Gordano,
e-mail**

DON'T waste money on expensive paper shredders to avoid having your identity stolen. Simply place a few dog turds in the bin bags along with your old bank statements.

**Ryan McCaffrey,
e-mail**

SAVE money on milk by not reporting your neighbour's death. You can even leave a note for their milkman to bring more expensive items like chicken or spuds.

**Mike Haskins,
Bristol**

LADIES. Save a fortune on expensive fashion magazines by flicking through the frock section of the Littlewoods catalogue and imagining your own facile, pointless editorial.

**Martin Christmas,
e-mail**

DON'T throw away old underpants. With the leg holes sewn up and filled with earth, they make smashing hanging baskets for trailing plants.

**A Titmarsh,
Harrogate**

BREAKFAST LOVERS. Make the 'toast always lands butter side down' myth wrong by dropping your toast, then quickly buttering it before someone sees.

**L.J.B.,
e-mail**

LEPRECHAUNS. Protect your finances by investing in a tracker fund, rather than relying on an ailing currency and leaving a 300-foot technicolour arrow in the sky pointing to where you have hidden it.

**David Goodall,
e-mail**

GIRLS. Embarrassing noises? Leave an empty trombone stand outside the lavatory door and people will think that you are just practising.

**A Non,
Lost**

HOUSEWIVES. Add Fairy Liquid to your recipes so you can cook and wash up at the same time.

**Sam,
e-mail**

KEEP your hands warm in the cold weather by cutting the finger tips off a pair of woolly gloves. These can be used as little warm 'hats' for each of your fingers.

*Steven Ireland,
Manchester*

WEATHER reporters Avoid overuse of the word 'treacherous' in your reports during snowy spells by investing in a bloody Thesaurus.

*Brian Patrick,
e-mail*

AUDIOPHILES. Eating 'space dust' while listening to your MP3 player adds that authentic crackly vinyl sound to your music.

*Chaddy McChad,
e-mail*

CHOCOLATE hundreds and thousands make ideal 'casualty' ants for ant action movie film directors.

*Sanny Sutherland,
e-mail*

VICARS. Increase the size of your congregation by substituting sour cream & chive Pringles at Holy Communion instead of the outdated unleavened bread wafers. I'm sure Jesus wont mind.

*Joderell Blank,
e-mail*

DIP the tops of leftover Yorkshire puddings into melted chocolate, then wait for it to harden and fill it with Angel Delight for a delicious council house eclair.

*Cora Flange,
e-mail*

BRITAIN'S 2.5M jobless. Why not retrain as Premier League football managers? Vacancies are always cropping up.

*Alan Mac,
London*

A SMALL bird tied by the leg to your ear with a short piece of string makes an ideal fan in warmer climates than this bloody shithole.

*M Coppereno,
e-mail*

AUSTRALIANS. Prepare for putting out this summer's bush fires by collecting and storing flood waters from Queensland.

*Owen,
Norwich*

DOG owners. Convince your pet that he or she is hard of hearing by silently mouthing the words 'walkies' and 'fetch.'

*Stewart Ferris,
e-mail*

ENVIRONMENTALISTS. Halve your carbon dioxide emissions by only breathing out once for every two intakes of breath.

*Dan Purvis,
e-mail*

SAVE money on correcting uneven floors at home by wearing orthopaedic shoes.

*Ed O'Meara,
e-mail*

USE PAPER underwear but don't throw it away after use. Simply use a rubber to remove skid marks.

*Graham Castle,
e-mail*

CREATE fun pub beer garden umbrellas for ants by pressing a few coloured drawing pins into a piece of plywood.

Darren Burke,
e-mail

TELL friends you've got access to Narnia by storing your Christmas tree in the back of your wardrobe.

Garreth Drummond,
e-mail

BEAR Grylls. When taking a helicopter trip, try sitting inside instead of out on the rails. It will be safer, much more comfortable and you won't have to shout.

Swiss Gary,
e-mail

GEEKS. When talking to someone face-to-face, simulate the shapes of emoticons using your facial muscles.

Stu,
e-mail

BRITISH comics. Send all your unsold copies of last month's issue to Australia, and call them the 'latest issue'. No one will notice, Christmas is in the middle of February over here.

Texas Pete,
Sydney, NSW

A DAIRYLEA triangle coated with Tippex makes perfect 'fun-size' Brie.

Chris Francis,
e-mail

OFFSET the carbon footprint of your daily car trip to work by driving home in reverse.

Bjorn Smorgesbord,
Sweden

LOOK at text upside down in a mirror. Hey presto! It looks like Russian writing, or something.

Phil Wadsworth,
e-mail

FORTNIGHT-OLD tortilla wraps make ideal Communion wafers for giant Christians.

Edward Barlow,
e-mail

A DR MARTEN boot with the bit that goes round your leg sawn off makes an ideal Dr Marten shoe.

Barney Farmer,
Lancaster

BRITISH Gas. When fitting new energy-efficient condenser boilers, don't bother spending a few minutes adding a quid's worth of lagging to the exterior outflow pipe. This will ensure further profits from emergency call outs to replace it when it inevitably freezes and bursts during cold weather.

TD Charles,
e-mail

REBOTTLED Smarties make ideal medication for hypochondriacs.

Sanny Sutherland,
e-mail

FARMERS. Instead of injecting your animals with hormones, improve the taste of the meat by injecting them with sauces, for example mint for lambs and gravy for cows.

Blarney O'Shite,
e-mail

TOPG TIPS

AFTER a hard night's drinking, eat two heaped spoonfuls of Bisto granules before going to bed and 'stir' by gyrating your waist. The following morning's inevitable bum gravy will be nicely thickened.

**Andrew McGuigan,
Stanley**

FILM makers. Why not cut down on the number of actors you need by having loads of identical twins and triplets in your stories, all played by the same actor, but never having them meet?

**N Scott,
e-mail**

ESTATE agents. Please look up the words luxurious, stunning and spacious in a dictionary so I don't have to spend my weekends being shown around badly-built shoeboxes.

**Simon Saladcream,
e-mail**

MEN. Re-create the excitement of a Soho peep show by going to a nudist beach wearing a burka.

**J. Geils,
Band**

DRIVERS. When overfilling your car with petrol by a few pence, simply wink at the assistant, laughingly telling her you'll "bring it in next time, love." This will put a smile on her face before her already meagre wage is docked. Again.

**Rosemary,
Billericay**

RACISTS. Convince others that you are not a racist by saying "I'm not a racist, but…" before saying something racist.

**P Dockar,
Leicester**

SAVE doing unnecessary ironing by putting on your shirt and tucking it into your trousers. Then, draw a line around the shirt at belt level with an indelible marker pen. The material below this line will never need ironing, thus saving time and effort.

**J.A. Colo,
e-mail**

A PEAR makes an ideal chicken leg substitute for vegetarians.

**W. Gamble,
Newcastle**

ITALIAN waiters. Embarrass men's girlfriends by making sexually suggestive hand movements with an enormous black pepper grinder whilst staring at their tits.

Greg Patterson,
e-mail

CAT OWNERS. Encourage your moggy to live a more active life by telling it that it died peacefully 8 times in its sleep.

Martyn Green,
e-mail

PUB chains. Microwaveable steak & ale pies and processed chicken make great accompaniments for tepid, flat lager.

Grant B Warner,
New Zealand

SURNAME Castle? Christen your son Warwick and save a fortune on personalised gifts by buying all his presents from the souvenir shop at Warwick Castle.

Greg Jackson,
e-mail

LONELY Guinness drinkers. Make friends with overworked bar staff near the end of a 9-hour shift by carefully explaining the correct way to pour a pint of the Irish alcoholic marmite.

Ali Brian,
e-mail

FAT people. Save money on expensive 'skinny jeans' by just buying jeans.

Mable Syrup,
e-mail

SAVE the price of one of those blankets with arms in by putting your dressing gown on backwards.

Mark O'Kane,
e-mail

KRAFT cheese slices can be used to make an attractive patchwork shoulder bag, sewn together using Cheesestrings. Use it for carrying cheese!

Edna Prolapse,
Mickleover

MODEL Railway Enthusiasts. Recreate the excitement of a 'Dastardly Whiplash'-style villain leaving a woman in peril chained to the railway tracks by exchanging your driver's cap for a top hat and cape and tying your tiny 'screaming lady' cock to a 2mm Standard gauge turnout track.

Christian Frank,
Billingham

PLACE chairs alongside the touchline at football matches so that if a mouse runs onto the pitch during the game, the female linesman can jump on one and scream her fucking head off.

Simon Picklewank,
e-mail

MODEL TRAIN enthusiasts. Save money on buying expensive model train sets by simply standing very far away from a normal-sized train station.

Alex Zeal,
e-mail

GIVE Monday mornings that Friday feeling by not turning up to work on Tuesday.

James Bailey,
e-mail

WOMEN. Make men do whatever you want by immediately following all orders with '...and I'll consider giving you a blow-job.' They never figure out that you don't really mean it.

Mrs A Fatliar,
e-mail

CHARITABLE People. Instead of buying the Big Issue, simply give the seller a house brick, roof tile or door handle, which can form the basis of a home-build project.

John Laing,
e-mail

MEN who are insecure about their sexuality. Cut bananas into little discs before eating them to prevent any unwanted thoughts.

Tom Dowling,
e-mail

DENTISTS. Save time telling patients to 'open wide' by simply showing really scary movies on a TV glued to the ceiling.

James Eadon,
e-mail

CAPRI-SUN drinks make excellent 'blood transfusion' bags for Jehovah's Witnesses.

Simon Ullyatt
e-mail

SOUTH Cambridgeshire bin men. Behind the hedge on the side of the road between Barrington and Haslingfield would be a great place to take a discreet shit if there were leaves on the hedge at the time.

Taig Knut,
e-mail

GEORGE Osborne. Don't get too depressed about your inability to function as Chancellor. Give it ten years and you'll be laughing about how you sold out to the banks and forced further millions into poverty on Have I Got News For You.

Jacksie,
e-mail

COMMUTERS. If you read the manual, you will find that your mobile phone was designed to REPLACE shouting.

Andy Mac,
e-mail

REBELLIOUS Arabs. Increase your chances of overthrowing a well-armed military dictatorship by not firing half your ammo into the sky every time you drive past a BBC camera crew.

Gaz Daffy,
e-mail

WHEN hosting sophisticated dinner parties, make all your guests drink out of the same glass, thus confusing CSI-style forensic teams in the event of someone being murdered.

Luke,
e-mail

ELECTRIC toothbrush manufacturers. Render your product totally useless by utilising the most sensitive of on/off switches, so that following any reasonable period of travel your £60 electric toothbrush will have turned itself into a £60 manual toothbrush by the time you've arrived and unpacked.

Bill Drummond,
e-mail

RECREATE a visit to the homeopath by simply drinking some tap water and throwing £50 out of the window.

Oli,
e-mail

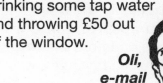

AN old plastic chicken packaging tray from Tesco can be placed upside down in your back yard to make an ideal 'eyesore civic building' for the ant community.

Emma Ness,
e-mail

MAKE fancy American root beer for your Fourth of July party by simply squirting Deep Heat into a bottle of Coke.

James O'Carroll,
e-mail

FOOL friends into thinking you have a passion for swimming by combing watered down bleach through your hair, and complaining of verrucas.

Fat Asp,
e-mail

WANT to know the time? Simply go to Argos and buy yourself a cheap watch. Hey presto! You should find the time printed on the till receipt.

Tomas Crauch,
e-mail

CALCULATE your body weight by standing on your scales wearing your shoes, note the weight, x. Then weigh one of your shoes and note the weight y. Your bodyweight, w, is then given by the equation w=x-2y.

Carrie Thortersen,
e-mail

SWAMIS. Avoid getting your feet blistered or burnt when fire-walking, by replacing your hot coals with Tesco Instant Light Charcoal Briquettes.

Spud,
Luton

24 DAYS before the clocks go back an hour, start putting your clock back an hour every night. That way you not only get an extra hour in bed for nearly a month, but you also gain a whole day. Or should that be 23 days before? Or 25? I can't do the maths.

Colin Smith,
e-mail

COMMUTERS. Instead of walking around with scalding hot buckets of watered-down coffee which you drink out of a tiny hole in a plastic lid costing you at least £2.50, I suggest you buy a kettle and wake up one minute earlier than normal and have a coffee at home like most normal people.

Javier,
e-mail

A GREYHOUND racing video, a picture of Basil Brush stuck to the telly and a kazoo makes an ideal fox-hunting kit for poor people.

Lenin G Radd,
e-mail

CAMPERS. Inflatable air beds make ideal ground-sheets 10 fucking minutes after blowing the fuckers up.

Carey Hunt,
e-mail

A McCOY'S crisp, painted silver, makes a realistic washboard for your Victorian dolls house.

Nisbet Crawford,
e-mail

SAVE money on parrots by instead buying a brightly-coloured dictaphone with a voice-activated replay function.

Monkey Boy,
Niontendo-on-Sea

John Humphries'
SHOP TIPS

SHOPPERS. Confuse staff at Argos by stealing all the biros and replacing them with IKEA pencils.
R. Trotter, Peckham

FEMALE shop assistants. When a garage mechanic comes to your till, add on a selection of random items they didn't know they needed, and charge them £50 labour costs for the transaction.
Tim Woods, e-mail

SHOPPERS. When you have finished and are leaving the supermarket, kindly offer your shopping list to people who are going in, as they may have forgotten to make one.
Kennon Baird, California

STAFF at the Orange shop in Camden. Save time and energy by leaving a sign in the window saying 'Call customer services on 150', then take the rest of the day off.
Dave Anderson, e-mail

SHOPKEEPERS. When selling booze, say to your customers 'It's Friday, it's 5 to 5…' and if they reply 'it's Crackerjack!' you don't have to check ID.
Pat Pending, e-mail

THRIFTY shoppers. Save cash when buying apples in the supermarket by removing the stalks to reduce the weight. You'll be smiling all the way to the checkout on your 176th visit as you effectively claim your free apple.
Will Mayes, e-mail

B&Q. Why not replace the ten permanently-unmanned checkouts in your stores with more sales shelving, giving your customers a wider range of products they can queue up for half an hour to pay for?
J Talia, North Wales

ALCOHOLICS. The foil bag from inside a wine box makes an excellent pillow to go to sleep on and provides a handy source for your 'Hair of the Dog' on waking.

Ben Cormack,
Castle Douglas

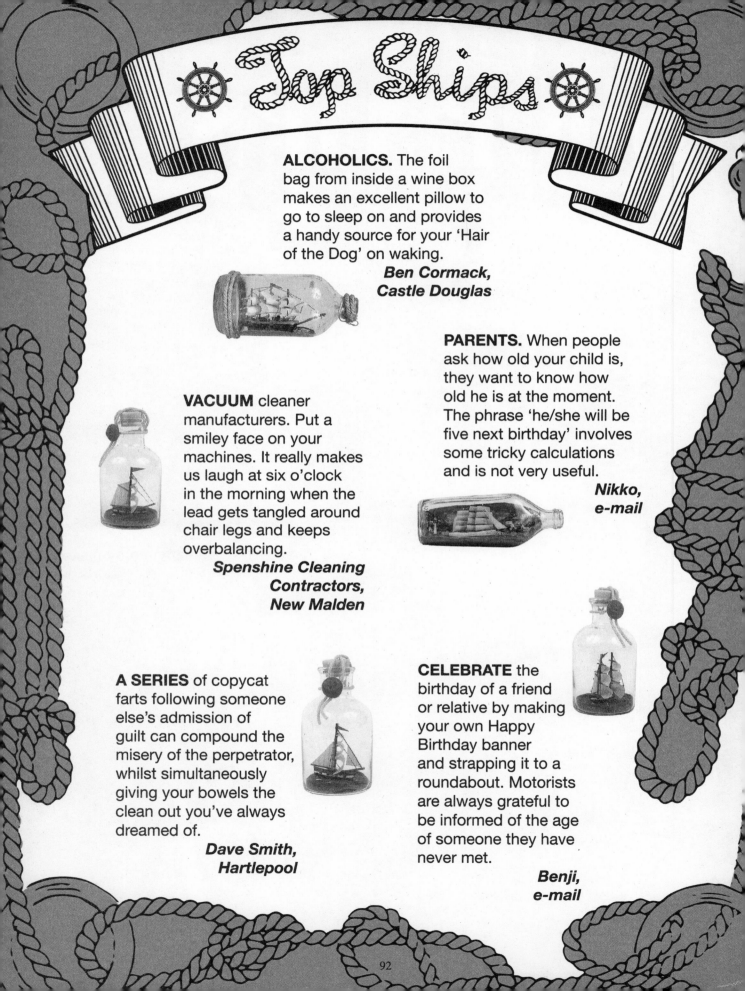

VACUUM cleaner manufacturers. Put a smiley face on your machines. It really makes us laugh at six o'clock in the morning when the lead gets tangled around chair legs and keeps overbalancing.

Spenshine Cleaning
Contractors,
New Malden

PARENTS. When people ask how old your child is, they want to know how old he is at the moment. The phrase 'he/she will be five next birthday' involves some tricky calculations and is not very useful.

Nikko,
e-mail

A SERIES of copycat farts following someone else's admission of guilt can compound the misery of the perpetrator, whilst simultaneously giving your bowels the clean out you've always dreamed of.

Dave Smith,
Hartlepool

CELEBRATE the birthday of a friend or relative by making your own Happy Birthday banner and strapping it to a roundabout. Motorists are always grateful to be informed of the age of someone they have never met.

Benji,
e-mail

DOGS. Forgotten which year you were born in? Simply take your age in dog years and divide it by seven, then subtract this number from the present year.

Jeffrey Dharma,
e-mail

JAZZ pianists. Screw up your eyes and face and shake your head about like you're Stevie fucking Wonder so everybody can see how amazing it all is.

Adam Gatward,
e-mail

LADY drivers, think of your car headlights as mood lighting rather than essential safety equipment. You may then switch them on.

Miggy,
e-mail

ALIEN abductees. Refrain from having a shit before going to bed even if you are touching cloth. That way, if you are abducted during the night, you can at least gain satisfaction from the knowledge that you have made a real mess of their anal probing equipment.

Matty,
e-mail

SATURDAY night party revellers. Please note that your kebab is not a reliable source of navigation.

Kyle,
e-mail

CHEDDAR and Mini Cheddar cheese biscuits make tasty replacements for lost 'Spirograph' drawing wheels.

Petesk8,
e-mail

MIXING gin with tomato ketchup makes an acceptable emergency Bloody Mary.

Tom Christy,
e-mail

BASTARDS. Convince your neighbour that he has developed tinnitus by hanging a wind chime in your garden where he can't see it.

Darryl Lane,
e-mail

FAT men. Next time you sit next to a swimming pool on a flimsy white patio chair, ensure that the camcorder is rolling. There could be 250 notes in it for you.

Bernard Pork,
e-mail

ENVIRONMENTALLY friendly lightbulb manufacturers. Get the jump on your competition by developing a product that converts electrical energy into light.

Simon Schunt,
e-mail

FOOL people into thinking that you used to have a tail by cutting a large hole in the seat of your trousers.

Sam B,
e-mail

STICK your fingers in both ears and simultaneously push them in and out rapidly to recreate the opening of 'Silver Machine'. Hey presto, an instant Hawkwind classic wherever you go, and no need for an expensive iPod.

T D Charles,
e-mail

JUSTIFY drinking alone by surfing Facebook at the same time. Hey Presto! You're now a social drinker!

Sari Simpson,
e-mail

LION tamers. Add extra excitement to placing your head in a lion's mouth by first putting a fruit pastille on its tongue.

Pud,
Leeds

DRINKERS. Avoid waking your other half when you come home inebriated by, over the course of the night, individually wrapping up all the coins in your pocket one by one in toilet paper and securing with an elastic band. This will eliminate any noise when they inevitably fall from your pockets whilst getting into bed. You may also want to mark the denomination on each one with a black felt pen to save unwrapping them all again whilst looking for your taxi fare.

**T. Dogshit,
e-mail**

WAIT until your wife has major dental surgery and then ask for a blow job. With all the anaesthetic it will feel like someone else is doing it.

**Baby Dave,
Derby**

TIMES Online readers. Save yourself £1 per day by simply going to thesun.co.uk and reading everything in a received pronunciation accent.

**Major V Cuntingdon-Smythe,
e-mail**

RAMEKINS make ideal 'shot glasses' for dogs.

**Andy Spracklen,
e-mail**

WHEN visiting Thailand, avoid getting tricked into taking a Ladyboy back to your hotel by first asking them to throw a tennis ball over-arm.

**Grant B Warner,
New Zealand**

CONVINCE your downstairs neighbours that you have a new subwoofer by simply stamping on the floor in time with the music you're listening to.

**Chris Kelly,
e-mail**

SAVE space in your freezer by storing frozen peas in the holes in potato waffles.

**Richard Vaughan,
e-mail**

CONVINCE colleagues you're Andy Murray by bringing your mum and girlfriend to work with you.

**Sexton Hardcastle,
Berlin**

WEDNESDAY night 5-a-side footy players. Avoid playing in the same team as someone with the same name as you. Alternatively, don't be upset when, in order to identify you from your namesake, you are referred to as 'Fat Paul', to pick a name entirely at random.

**Grant Cunningham,
e-mail**

RECREATE the thrill of riding in the Grand National by simply climbing onto your garden shed, putting your hands in your pockets and then leaping onto the ground below. If your collar-bone hasn't already smashed, try running into a nearby fence to make sure.

**Willy Wonky,
e-mail**

CATS. Annoy your owner by being the reason they don't take their dream job in America then scratch the fuck out of the new leather chair they bought themselves as a consolation.

**Clive Seatbelt,
e-mail**

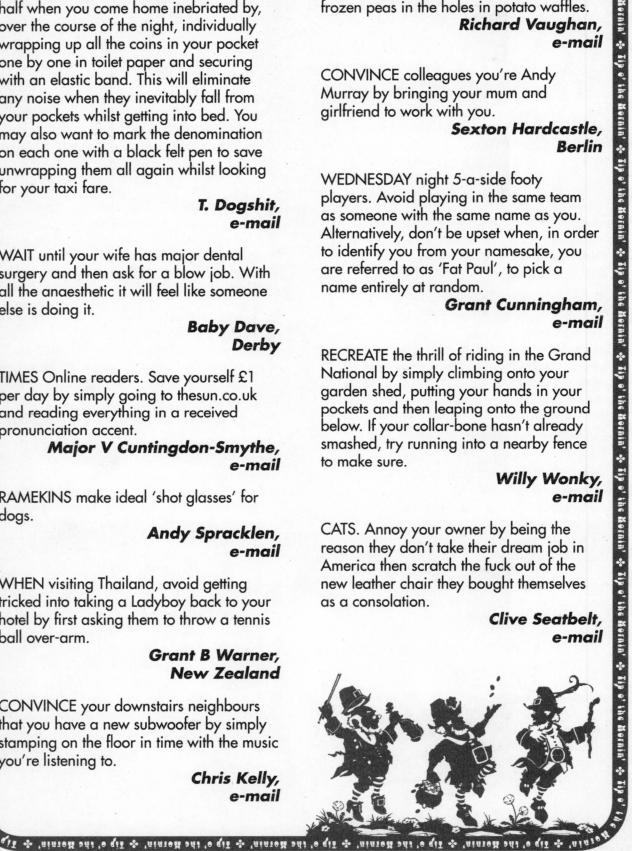

Tip o' the Mornin' ❖ Tip o' the Mornin' ❖ Tip o' the Mornin' ❖ Tip o' the Mornin' ❖ Tip o' the Mornin' ❖ Tip o' the Mornin'

94